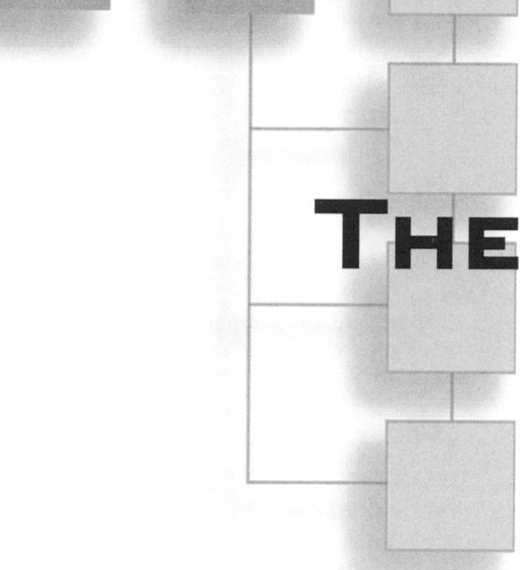

The Language of SQL

Larry Rockoff

Course Technology PTR
A part of Cengage Learning

Australia • Brazil • Japan • Korea • Mexico • Singapore • Spain • United Kingdom • United States

COURSE TECHNOLOGY
CENGAGE Learning™

The Language of SQL

Larry Rockoff

Publisher and General Manager, Course Technology PTR: Stacy L. Hiquet

Associate Director of Marketing: Sarah Panella

Manager of Editorial Services: Heather Talbot

Marketing Manager: Mark Hughes

Acquisitions Editor: Mitzi Koontz

Project and Copy Editor: Marta Justak

Technical Reviewer: Keith Davenport

Interior Layout Tech: MPS Limited, A Macmillan Company

Cover Designer: Luke Fletcher

Indexer: Valerie Haynes Perry

Proofreader: Chris Small

Library of Congress Control Number: 2010925128

ISBN-13: 978-1-4354-5751-5

ISBN-10: 1-4354-5751-X

Course Technology, a part of Cengage Learning
20 Channel Center Street
Boston, MA 02210
USA

Cengage Learning is a leading provider of customized learning solutions with office locations around the globe, including Singapore, the United Kingdom, Australia, Mexico, Brazil, and Japan. Locate your local office at: **international.cengage.com/region**

Cengage Learning products are represented in Canada by Nelson Education, Ltd.

For your lifelong learning solutions, visit **courseptr.com**

Visit our corporate website at **cengage.com**

Printed in the United States of America
1 2 3 4 5 6 7 12 11 10

For Lisa

Acknowledgments

As noted in the 2002 hit movie *About a Boy,* no man is an island. While that sentiment is certainly a general truth, it is one that I have specifically experienced as I've written this book. As such, I would like to acknowledge the help received from those who assisted, either directly or indirectly, with the words found between these covers.

First, I would like to thank the many editors at Cengage Learning who skillfully enhanced and improved many aspects of this book as it was brought to fruition. Without Mitzi Koontz, my acquisitions editor, this book literally would not exist. Keith Davenport, my technical editor, did an outstanding job in his review. I thank him for the numerous suggestions and corrections that he provided. Finally, Marta Justak, my project editor was superb in pulling it all together, while adding a professional touch and coherency to the entire project.

I would also like to thank a former colleague, Mary Anne Schneider, who contributed to my understanding of SQL, and other associates at ASAP Software who gave me the freedom to explore things on my own.

Finally, and most especially, I would like to thank everyone in my immediate family for their encouragement and support as I've dedicated myself to this project... this is for Lisa, Steve, Dan, Emily, and Kyle.

About the Author

Larry Rockoff has been involved with SQL and Business Intelligence (BI) development for many years. His main area of expertise is with data warehouse systems and reporting tools. He recently developed a suite of BI tools for ASAP Software, a subsidiary of Dell Inc. He holds an MBA from the University of Chicago, with a specialization in Management Science.

For more information on his current activities or to contact the author, please visit LarryRockoff.com.

Contents

Introduction

Research has shown that, being pressed for time, most readers tend to skip the introduction of any book they happen to read and then proceed immediately to the first real chapter.

With that fact firmly in mind, we will only cover relatively unimportant material in the introduction, such as an explanation of what you *will* and *will not* learn by reading this book.

On second thought, perhaps the introduction really *is* relevant, so you might as well stick with it. We'll make it brief.

Even if you're not yet familiar with SQL, suffice it to say that it is a complex language with many components and features. In this book, we're going to focus on one main topic:

- How to use SQL to retrieve data from a database

To a lesser extent, we will also cover:

- How to update data in a database
- How to build and maintain databases
- How to design relational databases
- Strategies for displaying data after it has been retrieved

A number of features make this book unique among introductory SQL books:

- **You will not be required to download software or sit with a computer as you read the text.**

  Our intent is to provide examples of SQL usage that can be understood simply by reading the book. The text includes small data samples that will allow you to see clearly how SQL statements work.

- **A language-based approach is employed to enable you to learn SQL as you would learn English.**

  Topics are organized in an intuitive and logical sequence. SQL keywords are introduced one at a time, allowing you to build on your prior understanding as you encounter new words and concepts.

- **This book covers the syntax of three widely used databases: Microsoft SQL Server, MySQL, and Oracle.**

  If there are any differences between the three databases, the Microsoft SQL Server syntax is shown in the main text. Special "Database Differences" boxes show and explain any variations in the syntax for MySQL or Oracle.

- **An emphasis is given to relevant aspects of SQL for retrieving data.**

  This approach is useful for those who only need to use SQL in conjunction with a reporting tool.

  Additionally, a final chapter is provided that covers strategies for displaying data after it has been retrieved, including ideas on how to use crosstab reports and pivot tables.

Finally, one additional question that we'll address in the introduction: How is SQL pronounced?

There are actually two choices. One option is to simply say it as individual letters, like "S-Q-L." Another possibility is to pronounce it as "sequel." There are people who claim that only one of the two pronunciations is correct, but there is no real agreement on the question. It's basically a matter of personal preference.

As for what the letters S-Q-L mean, most agree that they stand for "structured query language." However, there are a few people who will argue that SQL stands for nothing at all since the language is derived from an old language from IBM called sequel, which *did not* stand for structured query language.

At any rate, the introduction is done. And now . . . on to some real information.

Companion Web Site Downloads

Please see Appendix D, for a description of the files available on the companion Web site. These files list all SQL statements and provide all data shown in the book.

You may download the companion Web site files from www.courseptr.com/downloads.

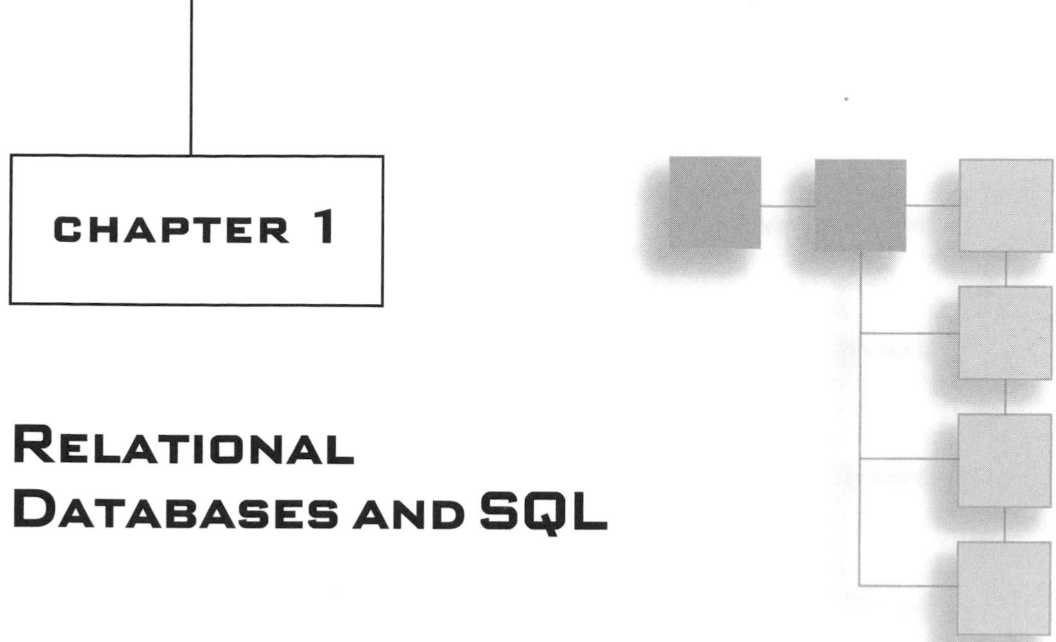

Chapter 1

Relational Databases and SQL

In this first chapter, I'm going to provide a bit of background that will allow you to get started quickly with the writing of SQL statements in subsequent chapters. There are two general topics. The first will be an overview of the databases covered in this book and some basic information on how those databases relate to the language of SQL. I'll also talk about the features of this book, which will allow you to determine readily the SQL syntax for the specific database you're using.

Second, I'm going to cover some of the key design features of relational databases. We'll talk about tables, rows, columns, keys, and datatypes. After you have the basic information, you'll be up and running in no time. So, without further ado, let us begin.

Language and Logic

I must begin with an admission that the title of this book is not entirely appropriate. Although the book is entitled *The Language of SQL*, a more apt title might have been *The Logic of SQL*. This is because, like all computer languages, the language of SQL has much more to do with cold, hard logic than with English vocabulary.

Nevertheless, there is a unique language-based syntax present in SQL that distinguishes it from many other computer languages. Unlike many programming tools, SQL employs ordinary English words such as `WHERE`, `FROM`, and `HAVING` as keywords in its syntax. As a result, SQL is much less cryptic than other languages you might have seen.

As such, after you become familiar with the language of SQL, you might find yourself thinking of SQL commands as being analogous to English sentences and having a certain expressive meaning.

For example, compare this sentence:

```
I would like a hamburger and fries from your value menu,
and make it to go.
```

with this SQL statement:

```
Select city, state
from customers
order by state
```

I'll get into the details later, but this SQL statement means that you want the city and state fields from a customer's table in your database, and you want the results sorted by state.

In both cases, you're specifying which items you want (hamburger/fries or city/state), where you want it from (value menu or customer's table), and some extra instructions (make it to go or sort the results by state).

So an important goal of this book is to allow you to learn SQL as you would learn English, in a simple, intuitive way. My approach will be to introduce one word at a time, while building on the logical intent and meaning of the language.

There is a second and perhaps less obvious meaning to the title of this book. There is often some confusion between the *language* of SQL and SQL *databases.* There are many software companies selling database management systems (DBMS) software. In common usage, the databases in these types of software packages are often referred to as *SQL databases,* since the SQL language is the primary means of managing and accessing data in these databases. Some vendors even use the word *SQL* as part of the database name. For example, Microsoft calls its latest DBMS *SQL Server 2008.*

But, in point of fact, SQL is more properly a language. It is not really a database. My focus in this book will be on the language of SQL rather than on any particular database.

SQL Defined

So what is SQL? In a nutshell, SQL is a standard computer language for maintaining and utilizing data in relational databases. Put simply, SQL is a language that lets users interact with relational databases. It has a long history of development by various organizations going back to the 1970s. In 1986, the American National Standards Institute (ANSI) published its first set of standards regarding the language, and it has gone through several revisions since that time.

Generally speaking, there are three major components of the SQL language. The first is called *DML,* or *Data Manipulation Language.* This module of the language allows you to retrieve, update, add, or delete data in a database. The second component is called *DDL,* or *Data Definition Language.* DDL enables you to create and modify the database itself. For example, DDL provides `ALTER` statements, which let you modify the design of tables in a database. Finally, the third component, *DCL,* or *Data Control Language,* maintains proper security for the database.

Many of the major software vendors, such as Microsoft and Oracle, have adapted the standard for their own purposes and have added numerous extensions and modifications to the language. But although each vendor has its own unique interpretation of SQL, there is still an underlying base language, which is pretty much the same for all vendors. That is what we will be covering in this book.

As a computer language, SQL is different than other languages you may be familiar with, such as Visual Basic or C++. Other languages tend to be procedural in nature. That means that they allow you to specify particular procedures to accomplish a desired task. SQL is more of a declarative language. In SQL, the desired objective is often declared with a single statement. The simpler structure of SQL is possible since it is only concerned with relational databases rather than the entirety of computer systems.

Microsoft SQL Server, Oracle, and MySQL

Although my aim is to cover the core language of SQL as it applies to all implementations, I will also provide specific examples of SQL syntax. And since syntax does vary somewhat among vendors, I've decided to focus on the SQL syntax utilized by these three databases:

- Microsoft SQL Server

- Oracle Database
- MySQL

If there are any differences among these three databases, I'll present the syntax for Microsoft SQL Server in the text of the book. I'll then indicate any differences for MySQL or Oracle in a box such as the following:

DATABASE DIFFERENCES

A box such as this one will appear whenever I present syntax differences for Oracle Database or MySQL. The syntax for Microsoft SQL Server will appear in the main text.

The heading of the box will indicate if the note is for MySQL, Oracle, or both.

Microsoft SQL Server is available in several versions and editions. The most recent version is called *Microsoft SQL Server 2008.* Available editions run from a basic Express edition to a fully featured Enterprise edition. The Express edition is free but still has an abundance of features that allow you to get started with full-fledged database development. The Enterprise edition includes many sophisticated database management features, plus sophisticated business intelligence components.

Oracle is also available in a number of editions. The most recent version is called *Oracle Database 11g.* Like Microsoft, Oracle also offers a free Express edition of its database.

MySQL is an open source database, which means that no one single organization owns or controls its development. Although MySQL was purchased by Sun Microsystems in 2008, it remains one of the top choices for open source software. Sun Microsystems was later purchased by Oracle. As an open source database, MySQL is available on numerous platforms other than Windows, such as Mac OS X and Linux. MySQL offers its Community Edition as a free download.

When starting out, it is sometimes useful to download the database of your choice, so you have something to experiment with. However, this book does not require you to do that. This book has been written in such a way as to allow you to learn SQL simply by reading through the text. I'll provide enough data in the text that you can understand the results of various SQL statements without having to download software and type in statements yourself.

Nevertheless, if you would like to download the free versions of any of these databases, the first three appendices at the back of this book have some useful instructions and tips on how to do that. Appendix A has complete information on how to get started with Microsoft SQL Server. The instructions include details on how to install the software and execute SQL commands. Similarly, Appendix B covers MySQL, and Appendix C explains Oracle.

In addition, Appendix D points to supplemental material that lists all the SQL statements shown in this book in all three databases. As mentioned, we show all SQL statements in this book in the syntax of Microsoft SQL Server. In most cases, these statements also work in MySQL and Oracle, but there are occasional differences.

Most readers will find it completely unnecessary to download the software or view the additional material shown in Appendix D. The examples shown throughout this book are self-explanatory and don't require you to do anything else in order to understand the material. However, if you are so inclined, then feel free to take advantage of these extra features.

Other Databases

In addition to Microsoft SQL Server, Oracle, and MySQL, there are many other SQL database software implementations. Some of the more popular packages are the following:

- Microsoft Access from Microsoft
- DB2 from IBM
- Informix from IBM
- SQL Anywhere from Sybase
- PostgreSQL, which is an open source database

Of these listed databases, Microsoft Access is somewhat unique, and it's particularly useful for SQL novices who want to learn the language. In essence, Access is a graphical interface for relational databases. In other words, Access allows you to create a query against a relational database entirely through graphical means. The useful aspect of Access for beginners is that you can easily create a query in a visual way and then switch to a SQL view to see the SQL statement you just created. So you can try different things and quickly see what the corresponding SQL syntax looks like.

Another distinction of Access, compared to the other listed databases, is that it is a desktop database. As such, it has great flexibility. Not only can you use it to create a database that resides entirely in a single file on your PC, but it also allows you to connect to more complex databases created with other tools, such as Microsoft SQL Server.

Relational Databases

Let's look at the basics of relational databases and how they work.

Basically, a relational database is a collection of data, stored in any number of tables. The term *relational* is used to indicate that the tables are related to each other. For example, let's take the simple case of a database consisting of only two tables: Customers and Orders. The Customers table contains one record for each customer who has ever ordered. The Orders table has one record for each order placed. Each table can contain any number of fields, which are used to store the various attributes associated with each record. For example, a Customer table might contain fields such as First Name and Last Name.

At this point, it's useful to visualize some tables and the data they contain. The common custom is to display a table as a grid of rows and columns. Each row represents a record in the table. Each column represents a field in the table. The top header row normally has the field names. The remaining rows show the actual data.

In SQL terminology, records and fields are actually referred to as *rows* and *columns,* corresponding to the visual representation. So henceforth, we'll use the terms *rows* and *columns* rather than *records* and *fields* to describe the design of tables in relational databases.

Let's look at an example of the simplest possible relational database. In this database, there are only two tables, Customers and Orders. This is what these tables might look like:

Customers table:

CustomerID	FirstName	LastName
1	William	Smith
2	Natalie	Lopez
3	Brenda	Harper

Orders table:

OrderID	CustomerID	OrderAmount
1	1	50.00
2	1	60.00
3	2	33.50
4	3	20.00

In this example, the Customers table contains three columns: CustomerID, FirstName, and LastName. There are currently three rows in the table, representing William Smith, Natalie Lopez, and Brenda Harper. Each row represents a different customer, and each column represents a different piece of information about the customer. Similarly, the Orders table has three columns and four rows. This indicates that there are four orders in the database and three attributes for those orders

Of course, this example is highly simplistic and only hints at the type of data that could be stored in a real database. For example, a Customers table would normally contain many additional columns describing other attributes of a customer, such as city, state, ZIP, and phone. Similarly, an Orders table would ordinarily have columns describing additional attributes of the order, such as order date, sales tax, and the salesperson who took the order.

Primary and Foreign Keys

Note the first column in each table: CustomerID in the Customers table and OrderID in the Orders table. These columns are commonly referred to as *primary keys.* Primary keys are useful and necessary for two reasons. First, they enable you to uniquely identify a single row in a table. For example, if you wanted to retrieve the row for William Smith, you could simply use the CustomerID column to obtain the data. Primary keys also ensure uniqueness. In designating the CustomerID column as a primary key, this guarantees that this column will have a unique value for every row in the table. Even if you happened to have two different men both named William Smith in your database, those rows would have different values in the CustomerID column.

In this example, the values in the primary key columns don't have any particular meaning. In the Customers table, the CustomerID column contains the values 1,

2, and 3 for the three rows in the table. It is often the case that database tables are designed in such a way as to generate sequential numbers automatically for the primary key column as new rows are added to the table. This design feature is usually referred to as *auto-increment.*

A second reason for primary keys is that they allow you to relate one table to another easily. In this example, the CustomerID column in the Orders table points to a corresponding row in the Customers table. Looking at the fourth row of the Orders table, you'll notice that the CustomerID column has a value of 3. This means that this order is for the customer with a CustomerID of 3, who happens to be Brenda Harper. The use of common columns among tables is an essential design element in relational databases.

In addition to merely pointing to the Customers table, the CustomerID column in the Orders table can be designated as something called a *foreign key.* I'll cover foreign keys in detail in Chapter 18, but for now, just be aware that foreign keys can be defined in order to ensure that the column has a valid value. For example, you would not want the CustomerID column in the Orders table to have a value unless that CustomerID actually existed in the Customers table. The designation of a column as a foreign key can accomplish that restriction.

Datatypes

Primary and foreign keys add structure to a database table. They ensure that all tables in a database are accessible and properly related to each other. Another important attribute of every column in a table is a datatype.

Datatypes are simply a way of defining the type of data that the column can contain. A datatype must be specified for each column in every table. Unfortunately, there is a great deal of variation between relational databases as to which datatypes are allowed and what they mean. For example, Microsoft SQL Server, MySQL, and Oracle each have over 30 different allowable datatypes.

It would be impossible to cover the details and nuances of every available datatype, even for just these three databases. What I will do, however, is to summarize the situation by discussing the main categories of datatypes that are common to most databases. Once you understand the important datatypes in these categories, you will have little trouble with other datatypes you may encounter.

Generally, there are three important kinds of datatypes: Numeric, Character, and Date/Time.

Numeric datatypes come in a variety of flavors, including bits, integers, decimals, and real numbers. *Bits* are numeric datatypes, which allow for only two values, 0 and 1. Bit datatypes are often used to define an attribute as having a simple true or false type of value. Integers are numbers without decimal places. Decimal datatypes can contain decimal places. Unlike bits, integers, and decimals, real numbers are those whose exact value is only approximately defined internally. The one distinguishing characteristic of all numeric datatypes is that they can be included in arithmetic calculations. Here are a few representative examples of numeric datatypes from Microsoft SQL Server, MySQL, and Oracle.

General Description	Microsoft SQL Server Datatype	MySQL Datatype	Oracle Datatype	Example
bit	bit	bit	(none)	1
integer	int	int	number	43
decimal	decimal	decimal	number	58.63
real	float	float	number	80.62345

Character datatypes are sometimes referred to as *string* or *character string* datatypes. Unlike numeric datatypes, character datatypes aren't restricted to numbers. They can include any alphabetic or numeric digit and can even contain special characters, such as asterisks. When providing a value for character datatypes in SQL statements, the value always needs to be surrounded by single quotes. In contrast, numeric datatypes never utilize quotes. Here are a few representative examples of character datatypes.

General Description	Microsoft SQL Server Datatype	MySQL Datatype	Oracle Datatype	Example
variable length	varchar	varchar	varchar2	'Thomas Edison'
fixed length	char	char	char	'60601'

The second example (60601) looks like it might be a numeric datatype since it's composed only of numbers. This is not an unusual situation. Even though they contain only numbers, ZIP codes are usually defined as character datatypes because there is never a need to perform arithmetic calculations with ZIP codes.

Date/time datatypes are used for the representation of dates and times. Like character datatypes, date/time datatypes need to be enclosed in single quotes.

These datatypes allow for special calculations involving dates. For example, you can use a special function to calculate the number of days between any two date/time dates. Here are a few examples of date/time datatypes.

General Description	Microsoft SQL Server Datatype	MySQL Datatype	Oracle Datatype	Example
date	date	date	(none)	'2009-07-15'
date and time	datetime	datetime	date	'2009-07-15 08:48:30'

NULL Values

Another important attribute of individual columns in a table is whether or not that column is allowed to contain null values. A null value means that there is no data for that particular data element. It literally contains no data. Null values are not the same as spaces or blanks. Logically, null values and spaces are treated differently. The nuances of retrieving data that contains null values will be addressed in detail in Chapter 8.

Many SQL databases will display the word NULL in all capital letters when displaying data with null values. This is done so the user can tell that it contains a null value and not simply spaces. I will follow that convention and display the word as NULL throughout the book to emphasize that it represents a unique type of value.

Primary keys on a database can never contain NULL values. That is because primary keys, by definition, must contain unique values.

The Significance of SQL

Before we leave the subject of relational databases, I'd like to review a bit of history in order to give you an appreciation of the usefulness of relational databases and the significance of SQL.

Back in the Stone Age of computing (the 1960s), data was typically stored either on magnetic tape or in files on disk drives. Computer programs, written in languages such as FORTRAN and COBOL, typically read through input files and processed one record at a time, eventually moving data to output files. Processing was necessarily complex since procedures needed to be broken down into many individual steps involving temporary tables, sorting, and multiple passes through data until the right output could be produced.

In the 1970s, advances were made as hierarchical and network databases were invented and utilized. These newer databases, through an elaborate system of internal pointers, made it easier to read through data. For example, a program could read a record for a customer, automatically be pointed to all orders for that customer, and then be pointed to all details for each order. But it was basically still the case that data needed to be processed one record at a time.

The main problem with data storage prior to relational databases was not how the data was stored, but how it was accessed. The real breakthrough with relational databases came when the language of SQL was developed, because it allowed for an entirely new method of accessing data.

Unlike earlier data retrieval methods, SQL permitted the user to access a large set of data at a time. With one single statement, a SQL command could retrieve or update thousands of records from multiple tables. This eliminated a great deal of complexity. Computer programs no longer needed to read one record at a time in a special sequence, while deciding what to do with each record. What used to require hundreds of lines of programming code could now be accomplished with just a few lines of logic.

Looking Ahead

This chapter has provided enough background information about relational databases so that you can move on to the main topic, which involves retrieving data from databases. We have discussed a number of important characteristics of relational databases, such as primary keys, foreign keys, and datatypes. We also have talked about the possible existence of NULL values in data. We will add to our discussion of NULL values in Chapter 8 and return to the general topics of database maintenance in Chapter 18 and database design in Chapter 19.

Why is the all-important topic of database design held off until much later in the book? In the real world, databases are designed and created before any data retrieval is attempted. Why would I not follow the same sequence of events in this book? In short, I have found that it is much more productive to plunge into using SQL without having to worry about details of database design. In truth, database design is as much an art as it is a science. As such, the principles of database design will be much more meaningful after you're more aware of the details and nuances of retrieving some data. So we're going to temporarily ignore the question of how to design a database and jump right into data retrieval in our very next chapter.

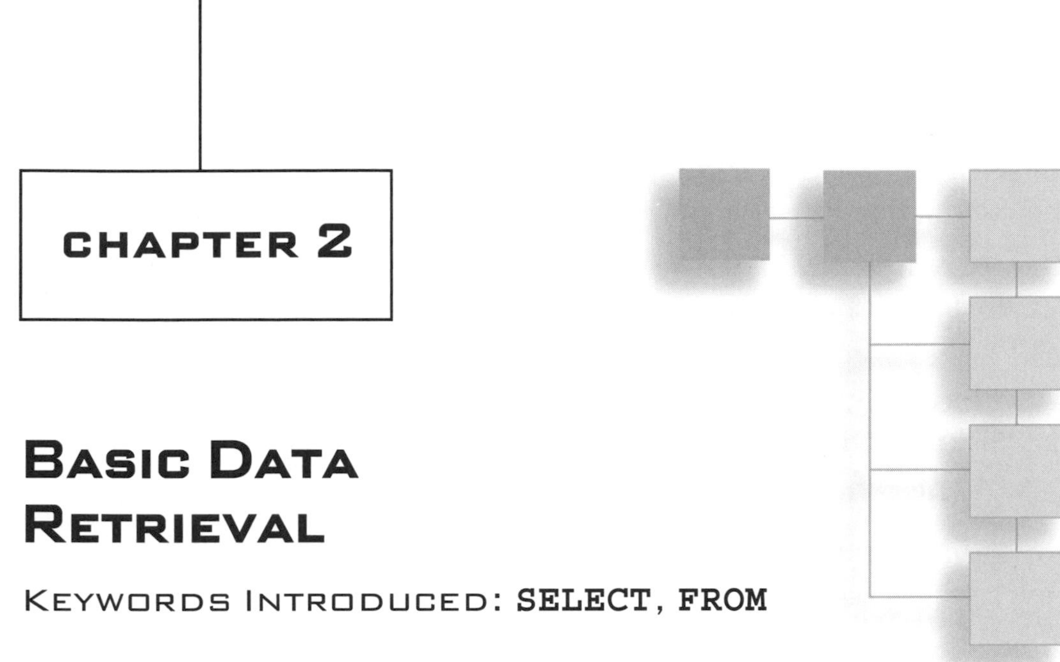

Chapter 2

Basic Data Retrieval

Keywords Introduced: SELECT, FROM

In this chapter, we are going to begin our exploration of the most important topic in SQL: how to retrieve data from a database. Whether you're in a large or small organization, the most common request made of SQL developers is the request for a report. Of course, it's a nontrivial exercise to get data into a database. But once data is in a database, the energies of business analysts turn to the wealth of data at their disposal and the desire to extract useful information from all that data. This is where the fun and usefulness of SQL begins.

The emphasis in this book on data retrieval corresponds nicely to the real-world demands that are placed on SQL developers. Your typical analysts don't care about how data gets into a database, but they do care about how to get something out of it. Your knowledge of SQL will go a long way toward helping your organization unlock the secrets of the data stored in their databases.

A Simple SELECT

The ability to retrieve data in SQL is accomplished through something called the `SELECT` statement. Without a lot of preliminary explanation, here is an example of the simplest possible `SELECT` statement:

```
SELECT * FROM Customers
```

In the SQL language, as in all computer languages, certain words are *keywords*. These words have a special meaning and must be used in a particular way. In this statement, the words SELECT and FROM are keywords. The SELECT keyword indicates that you are beginning a SELECT statement.

The FROM keyword is used to designate the table from which data is to be retrieved. The name of the table follows the FROM. In this case, the table name is Customers.

As is the custom, I will print keywords in all capital letters. This is done to ensure that they are noticeable.

The asterisk (*) in this example is a special symbol that means "all columns."

So to sum up, the statement means: Select all columns from the Customers table.

If the Customers table looks like this:

CustomerID	FirstName	LastName
1	William	Smith
2	Natalie	Lopez
3	Brenda	Harper

then this SELECT will return the following data:

CustomerID	FirstName	LastName
1	William	Smith
2	Natalie	Lopez
3	Brenda	Harper

In other words, it brings back everything in the table.

In the first chapter, I mentioned that it's a common practice to specify a primary key for all tables. In the previous example, the CustomerID column is such a column. I also mentioned that primary keys are sometimes set up to generate sequential numbers automatically in a numeric sequence as rows are added to a table. This is the case in the previous example. Most of the sample data I'll show throughout this book will show a similar column that is both a primary key and defined as auto-increment. By convention, this is generally the first column in a table.

Syntax Notes

Two points must be remembered when writing any SQL statement. First, the keywords in SQL are not case sensitive. The word `SELECT` is treated identically to "select" or "Select."

Second, a SQL statement can be written on any number of lines. For example, the SQL statement:

```
SELECT * FROM Customers
```

is identical to:

```
SELECT *
FROM Customers
```

It's usually a good idea to begin each important keyword on a separate line. When we get to more complex SQL statements, this will make it easier to quickly grasp the meaning of the statement.

Finally, as I present different SQL statements in this book, I will often show both a specific example and a more general format. For instance, the general format of the previous statement would be shown as this:

```
SELECT *
FROM table
```

Italics are used to indicate a general expression. The italicized word *table* means that you can substitute any table name of your own in that spot. So when you see italicized words in any SQL statement in this book, that is simply my way of saying that you can put any valid word or phrase in that location.

DATABASE DIFFERENCES: MySQL and Oracle

Many SQL implementations require a semicolon (;) at the end of every statement. This is true of MySQL and Oracle, but not of Microsoft SQL Server. For simplicity, I will show SQL statements without semicolons in this book. If you're using MySQL or Oracle, you'll need to add a semicolon to the end of your statements. Therefore, the previous statement would appear as:

```
SELECT *
FROM Customers;
```

Specifying Columns

So far, we've done nothing more than simply display all the data in a table. But what if you wanted to select only certain columns? Working from the same table, you might want to display only the customer's last name, for example. The `SELECT` statement would then look like:

```
SELECT LastName
FROM Customers
```

and the resulting data would be:

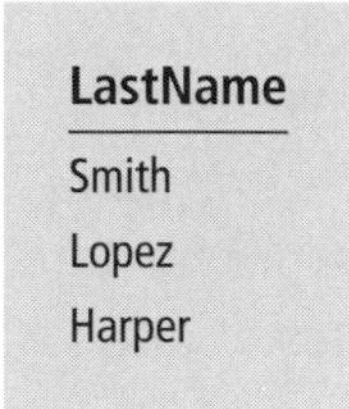

LastName
Smith
Lopez
Harper

If you want to select more than one, but not all columns, the `SELECT` might look like:

```
SELECT
FirstName,
LastName
FROM Customers
```

and the output would appear as:

FirstName	LastName
William	Smith
Natalie	Lopez
Brenda	Harper

The general format of this statement is:

```
SELECT columnlist
FROM table
```

The important thing to remember is that if you need to specify more than one column in the *columnlist*, then those columns must be separated by commas.

Also notice that we placed each column in the *columnlist* on separate lines. This was done to improve readability.

Column Names with Embedded Spaces

What if a column contains a space in its name? Let's say, for example, that the LastName column was specified as Last Name instead (with a space inserted between the two words). Clearly, the following would not work:

```
SELECT
Last Name
FROM Customers
```

This statement would be considered invalid since Last and Name are not column names. And even if Last and Name were proper column names, they would need to be separated by a comma. The solution is to use a special character around any column name containing spaces. The character to use differs, depending on which database you're using. For Microsoft SQL Server, the characters to use are square brackets, and the proper syntax is:

```
SELECT
[Last Name]
FROM Customers
```

One additional syntax note: Just as keywords are not case sensitive, it's also true that table and column names are not case sensitive. For example, the previous example is identical to:

```
select
[last name]
from customers
```

For clarity's sake, I will print all keywords in all caps and capitalize table and column names in this book, but that is not truly necessary.

DATABASE DIFFERENCES: MySQL and Oracle

For MySQL, the character to use around column names containing spaces is an accent grave (`). The syntax for the above example is:

```
SELECT
`Last Name`
FROM Customers;
```

For Oracle, the character to use around column names containing spaces is the double quote. The syntax for the example is:

```
SELECT
"Last Name"
FROM Customers;
```

Additionally, unlike Microsoft SQL Server and MySQL, column names surrounded by double quotes are case sensitive. That means that the previous statement is not equivalent to:

```
SELECT
"LAST NAME"
FROM Customers;
```

Looking Ahead

In this chapter, we've begun our exploration of how to use the SELECT statement to retrieve data. We learned about basic syntax and have seen how to select specific columns. In reality, however, this allows us to accomplish very little of a practical nature. Most significantly, we have not yet learned how to apply any type of selection criteria to our data retrieval efforts. For example, while we know how to select all customers, we don't yet know how to only select customers from the state of New York.

As it happens, I won't be covering selection criteria until Chapter 7. What will we be doing until then? In the next few chapters, we're going to build on what can be done with the *columnlist* component of the SELECT statement. In the next chapter, I'll be moving on to more variations on column selection, allowing us to create complex calculations in a single column. I'll also be talking about ways to rename columns to make them more descriptive.

Similarly, Chapters 4 through 6 will build on your ability to create even more complex and powerful *columnlists,* so when we finally get to the topic of selection criteria, you will have a full arsenal of techniques available at your disposal.

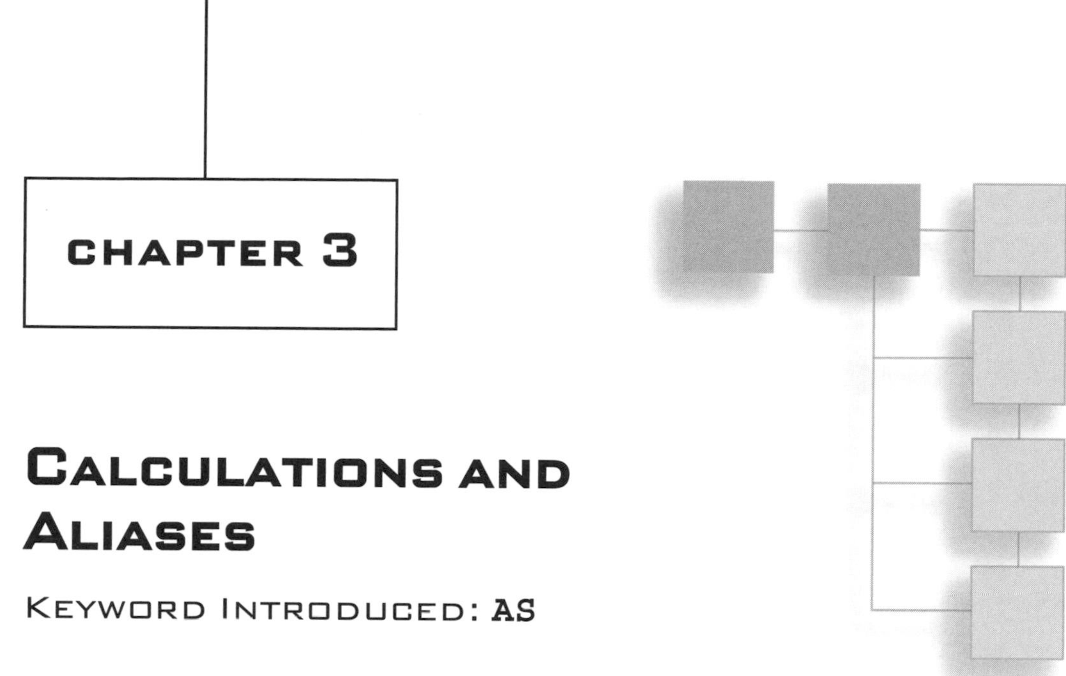

Chapter 3

Calculations and Aliases

Keyword Introduced: **AS**

The topics covered in this chapter will allow you to present information in a more convenient and interesting format for anyone viewing your data. The main technique to be discussed is known as *calculated fields*. This technique will allow you to perform calculations on individual data items that you retrieve from a database.

Using this approach, customer names can be formatted exactly as desired. Numeric calculations specific to your business or organization can be made and presented. As a SQL developer, you often need the ability to customize the content of individual columns in order to successfully turn data into more intelligent content. Calculated fields are very useful tools that can help you accomplish that goal.

Calculated Fields

When selecting data from a table, you are not restricted to the columns that happen to be in the table. The concept of calculated fields allows for a number of other possibilities. With calculated fields, you can do the following:

- Select specific words or values
- Perform calculations on single or multiple columns
- Combine columns and literal values together

Let's look at a few examples, all coming from this Orders table:

OrderID	FirstName	LastName	QuantityPurchased	PricePerItem
1	William	Smith	4	2.50
2	Natalie	Lopez	10	1.25
3	Brenda	Harper	5	4.00

Literal Values

Our first example of a calculated field isn't really a calculation at all. We're going to select a specific value as a column, even though the literal value has nothing to do with data in the table. This type of expression is called a *literal value.* Here's an example:

```
SELECT
'First Name: ',
FirstName
FROM Orders
```

This statement will return this data:

(no column name)	FirstName
First Name:	William
First Name:	Natalie
First Name:	Brenda

In this statement, we are selecting two data items. The first is the literal value `'First Name: '`. Note that single quote marks are used to indicate that this is a literal with character data. The second data item is the FirstName column.

Notice two things. First, the literal 'First Name' is repeated on every row. Second, there is no header information for the first column. When run in Microsoft SQL Server, the column header displays ("no column name"). The reason why there is no header is simply because this is a calculated field. There isn't a column name that can be used for the header.

DATABASE DIFFERENCES: MySQL and Oracle

Both MySQL and Oracle will return a value in the header row for literal values. In MySQL, the header for the first column in the previous example will appear as:

```
First Name:
```

In Oracle, the header for the first column will appear as:

```
'FIRSTNAME:'
```

One question you might very well ask is why the header row is important at all. If you are using the SELECT statement to bring back data in a computer program, then you probably don't care about the header. You only need the data. However, if you are using the SELECT statement to retrieve data for a report displayed to a user, either on paper or on a computer screen, then the header might be relevant. After all, when users look at a column of data, they generally want to know the meaning of the column. In the case of a literal value, there really is no meaning to the column, so a header isn't truly necessary. But in other types of calculated fields, there may be a meaningful label that could be applied to the column. Later in this chapter, we will discuss the concept of column aliases, which is a way of providing a header in this type of situation.

In addition to providing a column header where there is none, column aliases also allow you to change the name of a column to something that may be more meaningful for the person viewing the data. For example, a database designer may have given your last name column the obscure name of LstNm222. A column alias can be employed to change it to something more descriptive.

One more point about literals. You might think that all literals need quotation marks, but this is not necessarily true. For example, the following statement:

```
SELECT
5,
FirstName
FROM Orders
```

will return this data:

(no column name)	FirstName
5	William
5	Natalie
5	Brenda

Even though the literal value 5 is completely meaningless, it is still a valid value. Since it doesn't have quote marks, the 5 is interpreted as a numeric value.

Arithmetic Calculations

Let's return to a more typical example of a calculated field. Arithmetic calculations allow you to perform a calculation on one or more columns in a table. For example:

```
SELECT
OrderID,
QuantityPurchased,
PricePerItem,
QuantityPurchased * PricePerItem
FROM Orders
```

will return this data:

OrderID	QuantityPurchased	PricePerItem	(no column name)
1	4	2.50	10.00
2	10	1.25	12.50
3	5	4.00	20.00

The first three columns of the above SELECT are nothing different from what you've previously seen. The fourth column is a calculated column with this arithmetic expression:

```
QuantityPurchased * PricePerItem
```

In this case, the asterisk is a symbol that denotes multiplication. It doesn't mean "all columns," as was seen in the last chapter. In addition to the asterisk, several other arithmetic operators are allowed. The most common are the following:

Arithmetic Operator	Meaning
+	addition
−	subtraction
*	multiplication
/	division

Also note that, as with the literals, the fourth column has no header, due to the fact that it isn't derived from a single column.

Concatenating Fields

Concatenation is a fancy computer term that means to combine or join character data together. Just as arithmetic operations can be performed on numeric data, character data can be concatenated together. The syntax for concatenation varies, depending on the database you're working with. Here's an example from Microsoft SQL Server:

```
SELECT
OrderID,
FirstName,
LastName,
FirstName + ' ' + LastName
FROM Orders
```

The data retrieved is:

OrderID	FirstName	LastName	(no column name)
1	William	Smith	William Smith
2	Natalie	Lopez	Natalie Lopez
3	Brenda	Harper	Brenda Harper

Again, the first three columns are nothing new. The fourth column is this expression:

```
FirstName + ' ' + LastName
```

The plus sign denotes concatenation. Since the operation involves character rather than numeric data, SQL is smart enough to know that the plus sign means concatenation and not addition. In this case, the concatenation expressed is composed of three terms: the FirstName column, a literal space (' '), and the LastName column. The literal space is necessary so that William Smith doesn't display as WilliamSmith.

DATABASE DIFFERENCES: MySQL and Oracle

MySQL doesn't use a symbol (such as +) to denote concatenation, but it does require you to use a function called `CONCAT`. We'll be covering this function in the next chapter, but for now this is a taste of what the same statement looks like in MySQL:

```
SELECT
OrderID,
FirstName,
LastName,
CONCAT (FirstName, ' ', LastName)
FROM Orders;
```

Oracle uses two vertical bars (||) rather than a plus sign (+) to denote concatenation. The equivalent statement in Oracle is:

```
SELECT
OrderID,
FirstName,
LastName,
FirstName || ' ' || LastName
FROM Orders;
```

Column Aliases

In all the prior examples in this chapter, you have seen calculated fields with a nondescriptive header. We're now going to address the question as to how a header can be specified for these types of columns. The answer is to use a column alias. The term *alias* means an alternate name. Here's an example of how to use a column alias with the Microsoft SQL Server version of the previous `SELECT` statement:

```
SELECT
OrderID,
FirstName,
LastName,
FirstName + ' ' + LastName AS 'Name'
FROM Orders
```

Notice that the column alias of 'Name' is surrounded by single quotes. The output is:

OrderID	FirstName	LastName	Name
1	William	Smith	William Smith
2	Natalie	Lopez	Natalie Lopez
3	Brenda	Harper	Brenda Harper

The fourth column now has a header. The keyword `AS` is used to specify a column alias, which immediately follows the keyword.

DATABASE DIFFERENCES: MySQL and Oracle

The equivalent of the statement in MySQL is:

```
SELECT
OrderID,
FirstName,
LastName,
CONCAT (FirstName, ' ', LastName) AS 'Name'
FROM Orders;
```

Oracle does not require single quotes around column alias names. However, if the column alias contains embedded spaces, then double quotes should be used. The same statement in Oracle is:

```
SELECT
OrderID,
FirstName,
LastName,
FirstName || ' ' || LastName AS Name
FROM Orders;
```

In addition to providing a header for a calculated field, column aliases are often useful if a column in a table has a cryptic name that you'd like to change. For example, if a table has a column with a name of Qty, you could issue this statement to display the column as Quantity Purchased:

```
SELECT
Qty AS 'Quantity Purchased'
FROM table
```

Table Aliases

In addition to providing alternate names for columns, aliases can also be specified for tables, using the same AS keyword. There are three general reasons for using table aliases.

The first reason relates to tables with obscure or complex names. For example, if a table is named Orders123, you can use the following SELECT to give it an alias of Orders.

```
SELECT
LastName
FROM Orders123 AS Orders
```

Unlike column aliases, table aliases are not enclosed in quotes. When using table aliases, you have the option of using the alias as a prefix for any selected columns. For example, the above could also be written as:

```
SELECT
Orders.LastName
FROM Orders123 AS Orders
```

The prefix Orders has now been added as a prefix to LastName, using a period to separate the prefix from the column name. In this situation, the prefix wasn't necessary. However, when data is selected from multiple tables, the prefix will sometimes be required. This will be seen in later chapters.

DATABASE DIFFERENCES: Oracle

In Oracle, table aliases are specified without the AS keyword. The syntax for the previous statement in Oracle is:

```
SELECT
Orders.LastName
FROM Orders123 Orders;
```

Two remaining reasons for using table aliases will be covered in Chapters 11 and 14:

- Situations when selecting from multiple tables
- Situations when using a subquery in a SELECT statement

The meaning of the term *subquery* will become clear in Chapter 14 when the topic is covered in detail.

Looking Ahead

In this chapter, you learned about three general ways to create calculated fields in a `SELECT` statement. First, literal values can be used to select specific words or values. Second, arithmetic calculations can be used to perform calculations on single or multiple columns. Third, concatenation can be used to combine columns and literal values together. We also discussed the related topic of column aliases, which are often employed when using calculated fields.

In the next chapter, we'll be moving on to the subject of functions, which provide a slightly more complex way to perform calculations. As mentioned before, we're not quite at the point where you can apply selection criteria to your statements. I'm still building on the basics of what can be done with the *columnlist* in a `SELECT`. Don't worry. We'll get to the exciting stuff soon enough. In the meantime, your patience in sticking with this methodical approach will soon pay off.

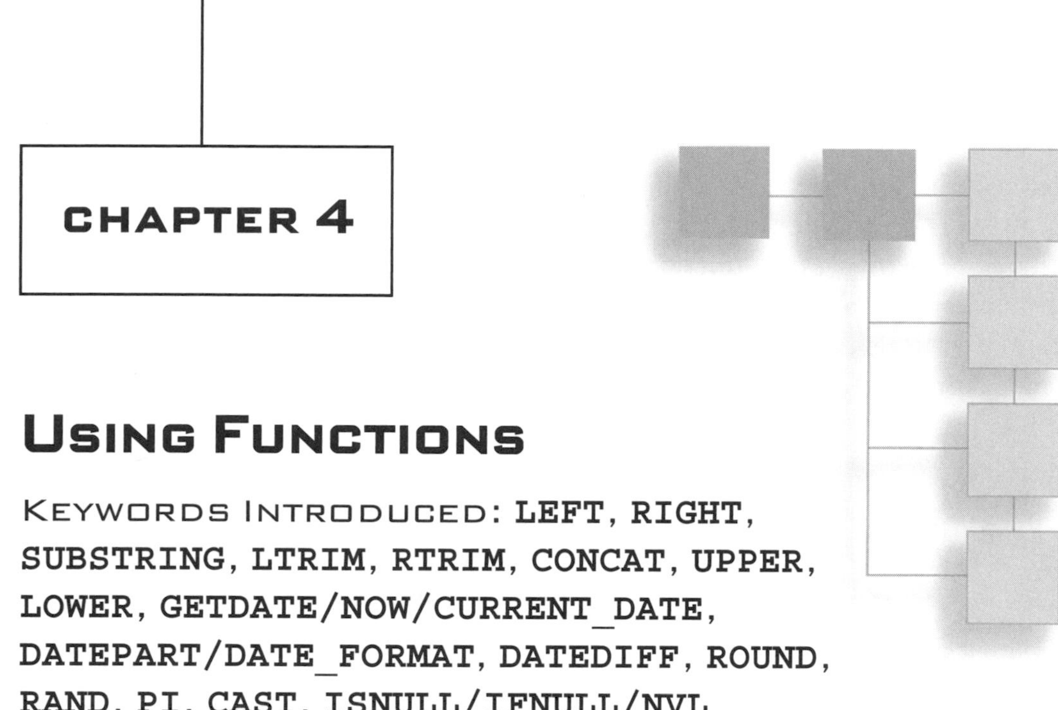

Chapter 4

Using Functions

Keywords Introduced: **LEFT**, **RIGHT**, **SUBSTRING**, **LTRIM**, **RTRIM**, **CONCAT**, **UPPER**, **LOWER**, **GETDATE/NOW/CURRENT_DATE**, **DATEPART/DATE_FORMAT**, **DATEDIFF**, **ROUND**, **RAND**, **PI**, **CAST**, **ISNULL/IFNULL/NVL**

For those of you familiar with spreadsheet software such as Microsoft Excel, you know that functions provide a huge amount of functionality for the typical spreadsheet user. Without the ability to use functions, most of the data available in spreadsheets would be of limited value. The same is true in the world of SQL. Your familiarity with some of the most commonly used SQL functions will greatly enhance your ability to generate dynamic results for those who will be using your reports.

This chapter covers a wide variety of some of the most commonly used functions in four different categories: character functions, date/time functions, numeric functions, and conversion functions. Additionally, we will talk about composite functions, which are a way of combining multiple functions into a single expression.

The Function of Functions

Similar to the calculations covered in the previous chapter, functions provide another way to manipulate data. As was seen, calculations involve multiple fields, either with arithmetic operators such as multiplication or by concatenation. In contrast, functions are often performed on a single column.

What is a function? A function is merely a rule for transforming a value (or values) into another value, using a specific formula. For example, the function SUBSTRING can be used to determine that the first initial of the name JOAN is J. There are two types of functions: scalar and aggregate. The term *scalar* comes from mathematics and refers to an operation that is done on a single number. In computer usage, it means that the function is performed on data in a single row. For example, the LTRIM function removes leading spaces from one specified value.

In contrast, aggregate functions are meant to be performed on a larger set of data. For example, the SUM function can be used to calculate the sum of all the values of a specified column. Since aggregate functions apply to sets or groups of data, we will leave our discussion of them to Chapter 10.

Every SQL database offers dozens of scalar functions. The functions vary widely between databases, in terms of their names and also how they work. As a result, we will only cover a few representative examples of some of the more useful functions.

The most common types of scalar functions can be classified under three categories: character, date/time, and numeric. Obviously, these are functions that allow you to manipulate character, date/time, or numeric datatypes.

In addition, you will learn about some useful conversion functions that can be used to convert data from one datatype to another.

Character Functions

Character functions are those functions that enable you to manipulate character data. Just as character datatypes are sometimes called *string datatypes,* character functions are sometimes called *string functions.* I'm going to cover these eight examples of character functions: LEFT, RIGHT, SUBSTRING, LTRIM, RTRIM, CONCAT, UPPER, and LOWER.

In this chapter, rather than retrieve data from specified tables, I'm going to simply use SELECT statements with literal values. Let's start with our first example, which is for the LEFT function. When you issue this SQL command:

```
SELECT
LEFT ('sunlight',3) AS 'The Answer'
```

it returns this data:

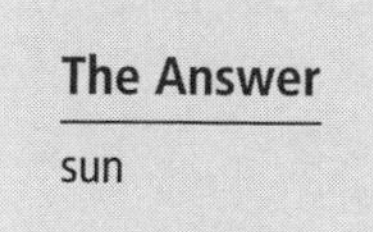

The Answer
sun

I included a column alias so the resulting data looks nicer. Note that there is no `FROM` clause in the `SELECT` statement. Instead of retrieving data from a table, you're selecting data from a single literal value, namely 'sunlight'. Strictly speaking, a `FROM` clause isn't necessary in a `SELECT` statement, although in practice, you would seldom write a `SELECT` statement like this. I'm writing the `SELECT` statement in this manner, without a `FROM` clause, only because it makes it easier to illustrate quickly how functions work.

DATABASE DIFFERENCES: Oracle

Unlike Microsoft SQL Server and MySQL, Oracle does require a `FROM` clause in all `SELECT` statements. If run in Oracle, all the examples in this chapter would require a `FROM` clause to be added. However, the table provided in the `FROM` clause does not have to be a real table. Oracle provides a special dummy table called `DUAL`. The use of the `DUAL` table will be illustrated later in this chapter.

Let's look at the format of this function in greater detail. The general format of the `LEFT` function is:

```
LEFT (CharacterValue, NumberOfCharacters)
```

All functions have any number of *arguments* within the parentheses. For example the previous `LEFT` function has two arguments: *CharacterValue* and *NumberOfCharacters.* The term *arguments* is a commonly used mathematical term that describes a component of functions and has nothing to do with anything being disagreeable or unpleasant. Basically, each function is unique, and the various arguments that are defined for each function are what truly define the meaning of the function. In the case of the `LEFT` function, the *CharacterValue* and *NumberOfCharacters* arguments are both needed in order to define what will happen when the `LEFT` function is invoked.

The `LEFT` function has two arguments. Other functions may have more or fewer arguments. Functions are even permitted to have no arguments. But even if there are no arguments, all functions have a set of parentheses following the keyword. The presence of the parentheses tells you that this is a function and not something else.

The formula for the LEFT function says: Take the specified *CharacterValue,* look at the specified *NumberOfCharacters* on the left, and bring back the result. In the previous example, it looks at the *CharacterValue* 'sunlight' and brings back the left three characters. The result is "sun."

The main point to remember is that for any function you want to use, you'll need to look up the function in the database's reference guide and determine how many arguments are required and what they mean.

The second character function is the RIGHT function. It's the same as the LEFT function, except that you're now specifying characters on the right side. For example:

```
SELECT
RIGHT ('sunlight',5) AS 'The Answer'
```

returns:

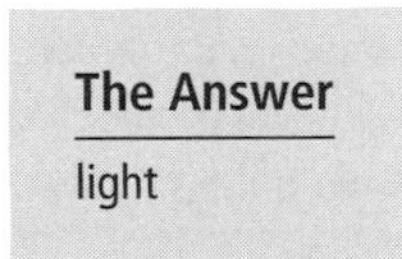

The Answer
light

In this case, you need to specify 5 as the number. If you used the number 3 instead of 5, you would have only gotten back "ght."

DATABASE DIFFERENCES: Oracle

Oracle does not provide the LEFT or RIGHT function. The equivalent functionality in Oracle is provided by the SUBSTR function, which will be discussed later.

You need to be aware of the fact that character data often contains spaces on the right. Let's look at this example, in which a table with only one row contains a column named President, defined as being 20 characters long.

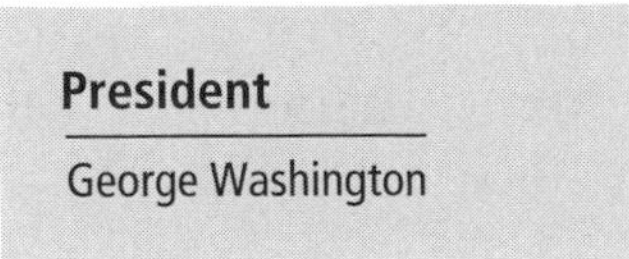

President
George Washington

If you issue this SELECT statement against the table:

```
SELECT
RIGHT (President,10) AS 'Last Name'
FROM table1
```

you will get back this data:

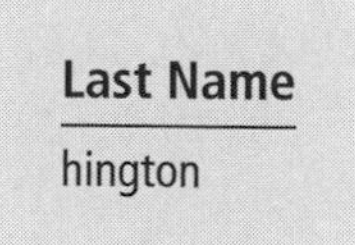

Last Name
hington

We wanted to get back "Washington" but only got "hington." Why? Because the entire column is 20 characters long. There are three spaces to the right of the value George Washington. So when you ask for the rightmost 10 characters, it's going to take the three spaces plus another seven characters from George Washington. You'll soon see that you need to use the RTRIM function to give you the data you're looking for.

You might be wondering how to select data from the middle of a value. This is done by using the SUBSTRING function. The general format of this function is:

```
SUBSTRING (CharacterValue, StartingPosition, NumberOfCharacters)
```

For example:

```
SELECT
SUBSTRING ('thewhitegoat', 4, 5) AS 'The Answer'
```

returns this data:

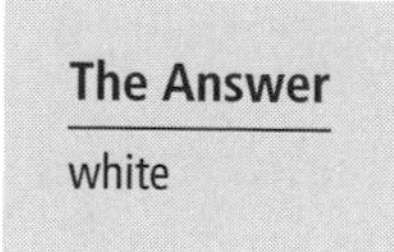

The Answer
white

This function is saying to take five characters, starting with position 4. Position 4 contains the w, so you end up with the word "white."

DATABASE DIFFERENCES: MySQL and Oracle

MySQL sometimes requires that there be no space between the function name and the left parenthesis. It depends on the specific function used. For example, the previous statement in MySQL needs to be written as:

```
SELECT
SUBSTRING('thewhitegoat', 4, 5) AS 'The Answer';
```

In Oracle, the equivalent of the SUBSTRING function is SUBSTR. One difference in the Oracle version of SUBSTR is that the second argument (*StartingPosition*) can have a negative value.

A negative value for this argument means that you need to count that number of positions backward from the right side of the column.

As mentioned, Oracle doesn't permit you to write a `SELECT` statement without a `FROM` clause. However, Oracle does provide a dummy table called `DUAL` for this type of situation. The equivalent of the `SELECT` with a `SUBSTRING` function is:

```
SELECT
SUBSTR ('thewhitegoat', 4, 5) AS "The Answer"
FROM DUAL;
```

Our next two character functions enable you to remove all spaces, either on the left or on the right side of a value. The `LTRIM` function "trims" characters from the left side of a character. For example:

```
SELECT
LTRIM ('the apple') AS 'The Answer'
```

returns this result:

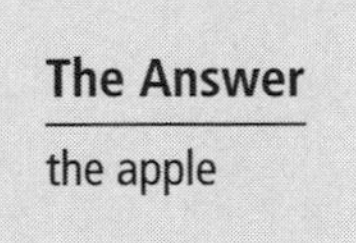

The Answer
the apple

The `LTRIM` function enables you to get rid of the spaces to the left of "the apple." Note that `LTRIM` is smart enough not to eliminate spaces in the middle of a phrase. It only removes the spaces to the very left of a character value.

Similarly, the `RTRIM` function removes any spaces to the right of a character value. An example of `RTRIM` will be given in the next section on composite functions.

The next character function is `CONCAT`. The `CONCAT` function discussed here is only available in MySQL and Oracle. As seen in the previous chapter, the plus (+) operator handles concatenation in Microsoft SQL Server.

Let's return to the concatenation example from the prior chapter. Our input data, from an Orders table, was:

OrderID	FirstName	LastName	QuantityPurchased	PricePerItem
1	William	Smith	4	2.50
2	Natalie	Lopez	10	1.25
3	Brenda	Harper	5	4.00

The syntax for concatenating the FirstName and LastName columns in MySQL with a `CONCAT` function is:

```
SELECT
OrderID,
FirstName,
LastName,
CONCAT (FirstName, ' ', LastName) AS 'Name'
FROM Orders
```

In this example, the `CONCAT` function concatenates the three indicated values: the FirstName column, a literal space, and the LastName column. The result of the previous statement is:

OrderID	FirstName	LastName	Name
1	William	Smith	William Smith
2	Natalie	Lopez	Natalie Lopez
3	Brenda	Harper	Brenda Harper

DATABASE DIFFERENCES: Oracle

The Oracle version of the `CONCAT` function only allows for two arguments. In other words, only two values can be concatenated at a time. To accomplish the concatenation in the previous example, a statement such as the following must be used:

```
SELECT
OrderID,
FirstName,
LastName,
CONCAT (CONCAT (FirstName, ' '), LastName) AS "Name"
FROM Orders;
```

This statement utilizes a composite function, a concept that is explained in the following section. In this example, the inner `CONCAT` concatenates the FirstName column and a literal space. The outer `CONCAT` concatenates that result with the LastName column.

The final two character functions to be covered are `UPPER` and `LOWER`. These functions convert any word or phrase to upper- or lowercase. These functions are sometimes helpful when presenting data. The syntax is simple and straightforward.

Here's an example that covers both functions:

```
SELECT
UPPER('Abraham Lincoln') AS 'Convert to Uppercase',
LOWER('ABRAHAM LINCOLN') AS 'Convert to Lowercase'
```

The output is:

Convert to Uppercase	Convert to Lowercase
ABRAHAM LINCOLN	abraham lincoln

Composite Functions

An important characteristic of functions, whether they are character, mathematical, or date/time, is that two or more functions can be combined to create composite functions. A composite function with two functions can be said to be a function of a function. Let's go back to the George Washington query to illustrate. Again, you're working from this data:

President
George Washington

Remember that the President column is 20 characters long. In other words, there are three spaces to the right of the value George Washington. In addition to illustrating composite functions, this next example will also cover the RTRIM function mentioned in the previous section.

The statement:

```
SELECT
RIGHT(RTRIM(President),10) AS 'Last Name'
FROM table1
```

returns this data:

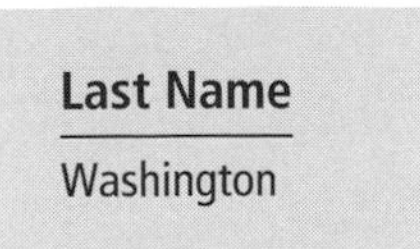

Last Name
Washington

Why does this produce the correct value now? Let's examine how it works. There are two functions involved: RIGHT and RTRIM. When evaluating composite functions, you always start from the inside and work your way out. In this example, the innermost function is:

```
RTRIM (President)
```

This function takes the value in the President column and eliminates all spaces on the right. After this is done, the `RIGHT` function is applied to the result to bring back the desired value. Since:

```
RTRIM (President)
```

equals "George Washington", you can say that:

```
SELECT
RIGHT (RTRIM (President),10)
```

is the same as saying:

```
SELECT
RIGHT ('George Washington', 10)
```

In other words, you can obtain the desired result by first applying the `RTRIM` function to your input data and then adding in the `RIGHT` function to the expression.

DATABASE DIFFERENCES: Oracle

As mentioned, Oracle requires you to use their `SUBSTR` function rather than the `RIGHT` function available in Microsoft SQL Server and MySQL. The equivalent of the previous statement in Oracle is:

```
SELECT
SUBSTR (RTRIM (President), -10, 10) AS "Last Name"
FROM table1;
```

Date/Time Functions

Date/Time functions allow for the manipulation of date and time values. The names of these functions differ, depending on the database used. In Microsoft SQL Server, the functions we'll cover are called: `GETDATE`, `DATEPART`, and `DATEDIFF`.

The simplest of the date/time functions is one that returns the current date and time. In Microsoft SQL Server, the function is named `GETDATE`. This function has no arguments. It merely returns the current date and time. For example:

```
SELECT GETDATE ( )
```

brings back an expression with the current date and time. Since the `GETDATE` function has no arguments, there is nothing between the parentheses. Remember, that a date/time field is a special data type that contains both a date and a time in a single field. An example of such a value is:

```
2009-07-15 08:48:30
```

This value refers to the 15th of July 2009, at 48 minutes and 30 seconds past 8 a.m.

DATABASE DIFFERENCES: MySQL and Oracle

In MySQL, the equivalent of `GETDATE` is `NOW`. The equivalent in Oracle is `CURRENT_DATE`.

The next date/time function enables you to analyze any specified date and return a value to represent such elements as the day or week of the date. Again, the name of this function differs, depending on the database. In Microsoft SQL Server, this function is called `DATEPART`. The general format of this function is:

```
DATEPART (DatePart, DateValue)
```

The *DateValue* argument is any date. The *DatePart* argument can have many different values. Some examples of valid values are year, quarter, month, dayofyear, day, week, weekday, hour, minute, and second.

The following chart shows how the `DATEPART` function evaluates the date '7/2/2009', with different values for the *DatePart* argument:

DATEPART Function Expression	Resulting Value
DATEPART (month, '7/2/2009')	7
DATEPART (day, '7/2/2009')	2
DATEPART (week, '7/2/2009')	27
DATEPART (weekday, '7/2/2009')	5

Looking at the values in the above chart, you can see that the month of 7/2/2009 is 7. The day is 2. The week is 27, because 7/2/2009 is in the 27th week of the year. The weekday is 5 because 7/2/2009 falls on a Thursday, which is the fifth day of the week.

DATABASE DIFFERENCES: MySQL and Oracle

In MySQL, the `DATEPART` function is named `DATE_FORMAT`, and it utilizes different values for the *DateValue* argument. For example, to return the day of the date '7/2/2009', you would issue this `SELECT` in MySQL:

```
SELECT DATE_FORMAT ('2009-07-02', '%d');
```

Oracle doesn't have a function comparable to `DATEPART`.

The final date/time function enables you to determine the number of days (or weeks, months, etc.) between any two dates. Again, the name of this function differs, depending on the database. In Microsoft SQL Server, this function is called `DATEDIFF`, and the general format is:

```
DATEDIFF (DatePart, StartDate, EndDate)
```

Valid values for the *DatePart* argument for this function include year, quarter, month, dayofyear, day, month, hour, minute, and second.

Here's a chart that shows how the `DATEDIFF` function evaluates the difference between the dates 7/8/2009 and 8/14/2009, with different values for the *DatePart* argument:

DATEDIFF Function Expression	Resulting Value
DATEDIFF (day, '7/8/2009', '8/14/2009')	37
DATEDIFF (week, '7/8/2009', '8/14/2009')	5
DATEDIFF (month, '7/8/2009', '8/14/2009')	1
DATEDIFF (year, '7/8/2009', '8/14/2009')	0

The above chart indicates that there are 37 days between the two dates. There are 5 weeks, 1 month, and 0 years between the dates.

DATABASE DIFFERENCES: MySQL and Oracle

In MySQL, the `DATEDIFF` function only allows you to calculate the number of days between two dates, and the end date is generally listed first if you want to return a positive value. The general format is:

```
DATEDIFF (EndDate, StartDate)
```

Oracle doesn't have a function comparable to `DATEDIFF`.

Numeric Functions

Numeric functions allow for manipulation of numeric values. Numeric functions are sometimes called *mathematical functions.* The functions we'll cover are ROUND, RAND, and PI.

The ROUND function allows you to round any numeric value. The general format is:

```
ROUND (NumericValue, DecimalPlaces)
```

The *NumericValue* argument can be any positive or negative number, with or without decimal places, such as 712.863 or −42.

The *DecimalPlaces* argument is trickier. It can contain a positive or negative integer, or zero. If *DecimalPlaces* is a positive integer, it means to round to that many decimal places. If *DecimalPlaces* is zero, it means that you want no decimal places. If *DecimalPlaces* is a negative integer, it means to round to that number of positions to the left of the decimal place. The following chart shows how the number 712.863 is rounded, with different values for the *DecimalPlaces* argument:

ROUND Function Expression	Resulting Value
ROUND (712.863, 3)	712.863
ROUND (712.863, 2)	712.86
ROUND (712.863, 1)	712.9
ROUND (712.863, 0)	713
ROUND (712.863, −1)	710
ROUND (712.863, −2)	700

The RAND function is used to generate random numbers. What is a random number and why would you ever need to generate one? This type of operation comes up when you need to select a random event, such as the winner among customers who entered a contest. The general format is:

```
RAND ([seed])
```

The square brackets around the *seed* argument indicate that this is an optional argument. The RAND function behaves differently, depending on whether or not the *seed* argument is provided. In most cases, the *seed* argument would not be used. If it's not used, then the RAND function returns a random value between 0 and 1. If executed 10 times in a row, it will return 10 different values. It looks like:

```
SELECT
RAND ( ) AS 'Random Value'
```

If the *seed* argument is specified, it needs to be an integer value. When the RAND function is executed with a *seed* argument provided, it will return the same value every time. It might look like:

```
SELECT
RAND (100) AS 'Random Value'
```

When you change the value of the *seed* argument, it will return a different value.

The PI function merely returns the value of the mathematical number pi. (Think back to your days in geometry class.) In reality, this function is very seldom used, but it nicely illustrates the point that numeric functions need not have any arguments. For example, the statement:

```
SELECT PI ( )
```

returns the value 3.14159265358979

DATABASE DIFFERENCES: Oracle

Oracle doesn't have functions comparable to RAND or PI.

What if you wanted the value of pi rounded to only two decimal places? Simple. You merely create a composite function with the PI and ROUND functions. You would first use the PI function to get the initial value and then apply the ROUND function to round it to two decimal places. The following statement returns a value of 3.14:

```
SELECT ROUND (PI ( ), 2)
```

Conversion Functions

All of the aforementioned functions relate to specific ways to manipulate character, date/time, or numeric datatypes. But you may need to convert data from one datatype to another or convert NULL values to something meaningful. The remainder of this chapter will cover two special functions that can be used in these situations.

The CAST function allows you to convert data from one datatype to another. The general format of the function is:

```
CAST (Expression AS DataType)
```

The CAST function is actually unnecessary in many situations. Let's take the situation where you want to execute this statement, where the Quantity column is defined as a character column:

```
SELECT
2 * Quantity
FROM table
```

You might think that the statement would fail due to the fact that Quantity is not defined as a numeric column. However, most SQL databases are smart enough to automatically convert the Quantity column to a numeric value so it can be multiplied by 2.

Here's an example where you may need to use the CAST function. Let's say that you have a column with dates stored in a character column. You would like to convert those dates to a true date/time column. This statement illustrates how the CAST function can handle that conversion:

```
SELECT
'2009-04-11' AS 'Original Date',
CAST ('2009-04-11' AS DATETIME) AS 'Converted Date'
```

The output is:

Original Date	Converted Date
2009-04-11	2009-04-11 00:00:00

The Original Date column looks like a date, but it is really just character data. In contrast, the Converted Date column is a true date/time column, as evidenced by the time value, which is now shown.

DATABASE DIFFERENCES: Oracle

The equivalent statement for the previous `CAST` function in Oracle is:

```
SELECT
'2009-04-11'AS "Original Date",
CAST ('11-APR-2009'AS DATE) AS "Converted Date"
FROM DUAL;
```

A second useful conversion function is one that converts NULL values to a meaningful value. In Microsoft SQL Server, this function is called `ISNULL`.

As mentioned in Chapter 1, NULL values are those for which there is an absence of data. A NULL value is not the same as a space or zero. Let's say that you have this table of products:

Product	Description	Color
1	Chair A	Red
2	Chair B	NULL
3	Lamp C	Green

Notice that Chair B has a value of NULL in the Color column. This indicates that a color for this chair has not yet been provided. Let's say that you want to produce a list of all products. If you issue this `SELECT`:

```
SELECT
Description,
Color
FROM Products
```

It will show:

Description	Color
Chair A	Red
Chair B	NULL
Lamp C	Green

However, users may prefer to see something such as "Unknown" rather than NULL for missing colors. Here's the solution:

```
SELECT
Description,
ISNULL (Color, 'Unknown') AS 'Color'
FROM Products
```

The following data is retrieved:

Description	Color
Chair A	Red
Chair B	Unknown
Lamp C	Green

DATABASE DIFFERENCES: MySQL and Oracle

The `ISNULL` function is called `IFNULL` in MySQL. The equivalent of the above statement in MySQL is:

```
SELECT
Description,
IFNULL (Color, 'Unknown') AS 'Color'
FROM Products;
```

The `ISNULL` function is called `NVL` in Oracle. The equivalent statement is:

```
SELECT
Description,
NVL (Color, 'Unknown') AS Color
FROM Products;
```

Additionally, unlike Microsoft SQL Server and MySQL, Oracle displays a dash rather than the word NULL when it encounters NULL values.

Looking Ahead

This chapter described a wide variety of functions, which are basically predefined rules for transforming a set of values into another value. Just as spreadsheets provide built-in functions for manipulating data, SQL provides similar capabilities. In addition to covering basic character, date/time, numeric, and conversion functions, I've also explained how to create composite functions from two or more of these functions.

A lot of the material on functions is necessarily dry, due to the fact that there are simply so many available functions with widely varying capabilities. It's impossible to discuss every nuance of every available function. The thing to remember is that functions can be looked up easily in a database's reference guide when they need to be used. Online reference material can serve as a handy resource for exactly how each function works. So when you need to use any particular function, you can simply check online to verify the function's syntax.

In our next chapter, we're going to take a break from *columnlist* issues and talk about something a little more fun—how to sort your data. Sorts can serve lots of useful purposes and satisfy the basic desire of users to view data in some sort of order. With the sort, we will begin to think of the entire way in which our information is presented, rather than with just bits and pieces of individual data items.

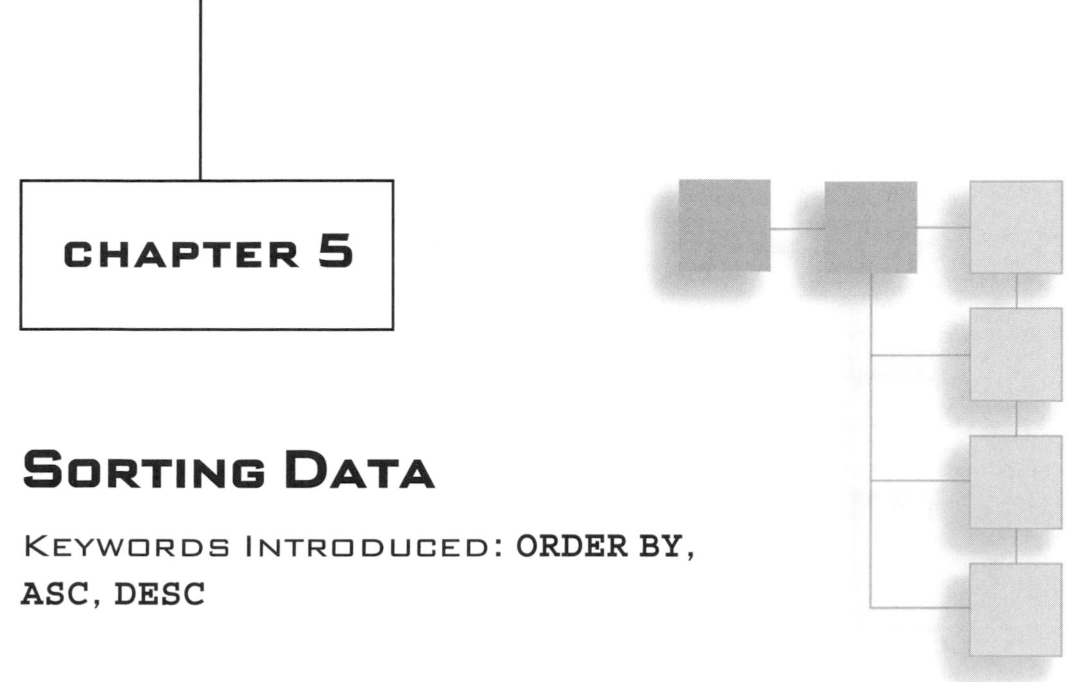

Chapter 5

Sorting Data

Keywords Introduced: **ORDER BY, ASC, DESC**

The ability to present data in a sorted order is often essential to the task at hand. For example, if you were shown a large list of customers in a random order, you'd find it difficult to locate any one particular customer. However, if the same list were sorted alphabetically, then you could quickly locate the desired customer.

The idea of sorting data alphabetically applies to many situations, even when the data isn't strictly alphabetic in nature. For example, you may want to sort a list of orders by the order date and time to allow you to rapidly find an order taken at a particular date and time. Or you might want to sort a list of orders by the order amount, to allow you to view orders from the smallest to the largest. No matter what particular form your sort takes, it adds a useful way to organize your data as it is being presented to the end user.

Adding a Sort

Up until now, data has not been returned in any particular order. When a `SELECT` is issued, you never know which row will come first. If the query is executed from within a software program, and no one ever sees the data at that point in time, then it really doesn't matter. But if the data is to be immediately displayed to a user, then the order of rows is often significant. A sort can be added easily to a `SELECT` statement by using an `ORDER BY` clause.

Here's the general format for a SELECT statement with an ORDER BY clause:

```
SELECT columnlist
FROM tablelist
ORDER BY columnlist
```

The ORDER BY clause is always after the FROM clause, which, in turn, is always after the SELECT keyword. The italicized *columnlist* for the SELECT and ORDER BY keywords indicates that any number of columns can be listed. The columns in *columnlist* can be individual columns or more complex expressions. The columns specified after the SELECT and ORDER BY keywords can be entirely different columns. The italicized *tablelist* indicates that any number of tables can be listed, although you have not yet seen the syntax for listing multiple tables.

Turning to an example, you'll be working from data in this Customers table:

CustomerID	FirstName	LastName
1	William	Smith
2	Janet	Smith
3	Natalie	Lopez
4	Brenda	Harper

Sorting in Ascending Order

If you want to sort data in alphabetic order, with A coming before Z, then you simply need to add an ORDER BY clause to the SELECT. For example:

```
SELECT
FirstName,
LastName
FROM Customers
ORDER BY LastName
```

brings back this data:

FirstName	LastName
Brenda	Harper
Natalie	Lopez
William	Smith
Janet	Smith

Since there are two Smiths, William and Janet, there's no way to predict which one will be listed first. This is because you are only sorting on LastName, and there are multiple rows with the same last name.

Similarly, if you issue this `SELECT`:

```
SELECT
FirstName,
LastName
FROM Customers
ORDER BY FirstName
```

then this data is retrieved:

FirstName	LastName
Brenda	Harper
Janet	Smith
Natalie	Lopez
William	Smith

The order is now completely different since you're sorting by first name.

SQL provides a special keyword named `ASC`, which stands for *ascending*. This keyword is completely optional and largely unnecessary since all sorts are assumed to be in ascending order by default. The following `SELECT`, which uses the `ASC` keyword, returns the same data as shown previously:

```
SELECT
FirstName,
LastName
FROM Customers
ORDER BY FirstName ASC
```

The keyword `ASC` is used to emphasize the fact that the sort is ascending, as opposed to descending.

Sorting in Descending Order

The `DESC` keyword sorts in an order opposite to `ASC`. Instead of ascending, the order in such a sort is descending.

For example:

```
SELECT
FirstName,
LastName
FROM Customers
ORDER BY FirstName DESC
```

retrieves:

FirstName	LastName
William	Smith
Natalie	Lopez
Janet	Smith
Brenda	Harper

The first names are now in a Z to A order.

Sorting by Multiple Columns

We now return to the problem of what to do with the Smiths. If you want to sort by last name, but there are two people with the same last name, you need to add a secondary sort by first name, as follows:

```
SELECT
FirstName,
LastName
FROM Customers
ORDER BY LastName, FirstName
```

This brings back:

FirstName	LastName
Brenda	Harper
Natalie	Lopez
Janet	Smith
William	Smith

Since you are specifying a second sort column, you can now be certain that Janet Smith will appear before William Smith. Note that the `ORDER BY` clause needs to list LastName before FirstName. The order of the columns is significant. Your intention is to sort first by LastName and then by FirstName, so you need to list the LastName column first.

Sorting by a Calculated Field

We're now going to throw in our knowledge of calculated fields and aliases from Chapter 3 to illustrate some further possibilities. This `SELECT`:

```
SELECT
LastName + ', ' + FirstName AS 'Name'
FROM Customers
ORDER BY Name
```

returns this data:

Name
Harper, Brenda
Lopez, Natalie
Smith, Janet
Smith, William

As seen, you are able to refer to a column alias (Name) in the `ORDER BY` clause. This illustrates another reason as to why aliases are often useful. Also, note the design of the calculated field itself. You inserted a comma and a space between the last and first name columns, to separate them and to show the name in a commonly used format. Conveniently, this format also works well for sorting. The ability to display names in this format, with a comma separating the last and first name, is a handy trick to keep in mind. Users very often want to see names arranged in this manner.

But what if you want to put the calculated field directly in the `ORDER BY` clause without also using it as a column alias? Similar to the above, you could also specify:

```
SELECT
FirstName,
LastName
FROM Customers
ORDER BY LastName + FirstName
```

This would display:

FirstName	LastName
Brenda	Harper
Natalie	Lopez
Janet	Smith
William	Smith

The data is sorted the same as in the prior example. The only difference is that you're now specifying a calculated field in the ORDER BY clause without making use of column aliases.

More on Sort Sequences

In the previous examples, all of the data is character data, consisting of letters from A to Z. There are no numbers or special characters. Additionally, there has been no consideration of upper- and lowercase letters. In an ascending sort, would the word "dog" appear before or after "DOG"?

Each database lets users specify or customize collation settings, which provide details on how data is sorted. The settings vary somewhat among databases, but three facts are generally true.

First, when data is sorted in an ascending order, any data with NULL values appear first. As previously discussed, NULL values are those where there is an absence of any data. After any NULLs, numbers will appear before characters. For data sorted in descending order, character data will display first, then numbers, and then NULLs.

Second, for character data, there is usually no differentiation between upper- and lowercase. An e is treated the same as an E.

DATABASE DIFFERENCES: Oracle

In Oracle, unlike in Microsoft SQL Server and MySQL, NULL values appear last in a list sorted in ascending order.

In Oracle, one can add a special NULLS FIRST keyword to the ORDER BY clause to force NULL values to appear first in an ascending sort. The general format for such a statement is:

```
SELECT columnlist
FROM tablelist
ORDER BY columnlist NULLS FIRST
```

If the `NULLS FIRST` keyword appears in a sort with a descending order, then NULL values will appear last, as they normally would.

Additionally, unlike in Microsoft SQL Server and MySQL, Oracle treats upper- and lowercase letters differently in a sorted list. In Oracle, uppercase letters always appear before lowercase letters in a list sorted in ascending order. For example, in Oracle, the word "DOG" will appear before the word "dog." In Microsoft SQL Server and MySQL, DOG and dog are treated identically.

Third, for character data, the individual characters comprising the value are evaluated from left to right. If we're talking about letters, then AB will come before AC. Let's look at an example, taken from this table:

TableID	CharacterData	NumericData
1	23	23
2	5	5
3	Dog	NULL
4	NULL	–6

In this table, the CharacterData column is defined as a character column, for example, as VARCHAR (a variable length datatype). Similarly, the NumericData column is defined as a numeric column, for example as INT (an integer datatype). Values with no data are displayed as NULL.

When this `SELECT` is issued against the table:

```
SELECT NumericData
FROM tablename
ORDER BY NumericData
```

it will display:

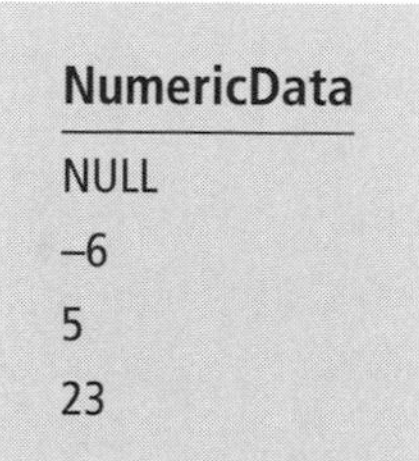

NumericData
NULL
–6
5
23

Notice that NULLs come first, then the numbers in numeric sequence. If we want the NULL values to assume a default value of 0, we can use the `ISNULL` function seen in the last chapter and issue this `SELECT` statement:

```
SELECT
ISNULL (NumericData, 0)
FROM tablename
ORDER BY ISNULL (NumericData, 0)
```

The result is now:

NumericData
–6
0
5
23

The `ISNULL` function converted the NULL value to a 0, which results in a different sort order.

The decision as to whether you want NULL values to display as NULL or as 0 depends on the specific application you're using. Basically, if the user thinks of NULL values as meaning 0, then you should display NULLs as 0. However, if the user sees NULL values as an absence of data, then a display of the word NULL is appropriate.

Turning to a different `ORDER BY` clause against the same table, if we issue this `SELECT`:

```
SELECT
CharacterData
FROM tablename
ORDER BY CharacterData
```

it will display:

CharacterData
NULL
23
5
Dog

As expected, NULLs come first, then values with numeric digits, and then values with alphabetic characters. Notice that 23 comes before 5. This is because the 23 and 5 values are being evaluated as characters, not numbers. Since character data is evaluated from left to right and since 2 is lower than 5, 23 is displayed first.

Looking Ahead

In this chapter, we talked about the basic possibilities for sorting data in a specific order. We illustrated how to sort by more than one column. We also discussed using calculated fields in sorts. Finally, we covered some of the quirks of sorting, particularly when it comes to data with NULL values and with numbers in character columns.

At the start of the chapter, we mentioned some of the general uses for sorts. Primary among these is the ability to simply place data in an easily understood order, thus allowing users to quickly locate their desired piece of information. People generally like to see data in order, and sorts accomplish that goal. Another interesting use of sorts will be covered in Chapter 7. In that chapter, we're going to introduce the keyword `TOP` and another way to use sorts in conjunction with that keyword. This technique, commonly known as a *Top N* sort, will allow you, for example, to display customers with the top five orders for a given time period.

In our next chapter, we're going to conclude our analysis of what can be done with *columnlists*. Using the `CASE` statement and column-based logic, we're going to explore ways to inject some real logic into our *columnlist* expressions.

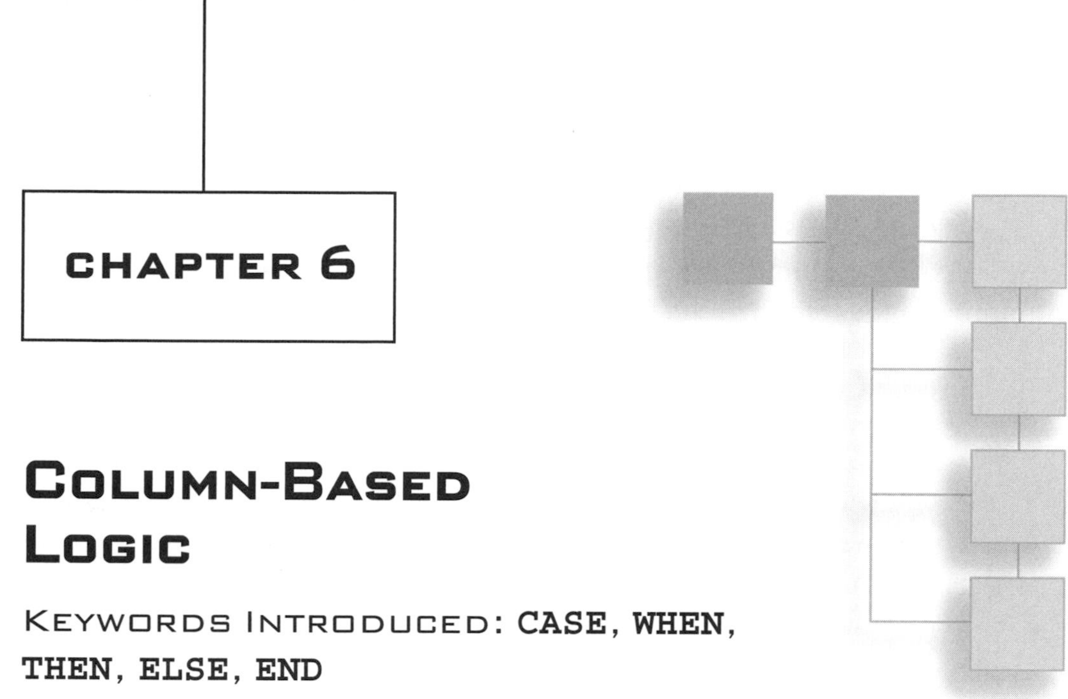

Chapter 6

Column-Based Logic

Keywords Introduced: **CASE**, **WHEN**, **THEN**, **ELSE**, **END**

The main topic of this chapter is something called the CASE expression. As indicated by the title of this chapter, CASE expressions are a form of column-based logic. That term is meant to indicate that these expressions apply logic to columns rather than rows. CASE expressions are also sometimes referred to as *conditional logic*. Basically, CASE expressions allow you to alter the output you present to a user based on a logical condition, as it applies to an evaluation of specific columns or data elements.

As a beginning SQL developer, you should know that the CASE expression is a relatively advanced topic. You can get by without ever using CASE expressions and still write some useful queries. But your knowledge of this topic is the type of thing that can really set you apart. In fact, after you've gone through the entire book, this is one of the topics you may want to review again, to get you thinking about some of the interesting things that can be accomplished with this technique.

IF-THEN-ELSE Logic

Let's turn to some honest-to-goodness logic next. Up until now, you've learned how to select columns from a single table, apply some calculations and functions, and add a sort. However, you have not yet done anything all that logical.

The CASE expression in SQL enables you to apply a traditional IF-THEN-ELSE type of logic to a single expression in a SELECT statement. The term *IF-THEN-ELSE* refers to a commonly used logical construct employed by procedural programming languages. In general terms, this type of logic looks like:

```
IF some condition is true
THEN do this
ELSE do that
```

A CASE expression is a construct that can appear in a number of places in a SELECT statement. In this chapter, we're going to focus on CASE expressions that appear within the *columnlist* immediately following the SELECT keyword. A SELECT statement that includes both columns and a CASE expression might look like this:

```
SELECT
column1,
column2,
CaseExpression
FROM table
```

The Simple Format

There are two general formats for the CASE expression, generally referred to as *simple* and *searched.* The simple format is:

```
SELECT
CASE ColumnOrExpression
WHEN value1 THEN result1
WHEN value2 THEN result2
(repeat WHEN-THEN any number of times)
[ELSE DefaultResult]
END
```

As can be seen, the CASE expression utilizes a number of keywords other than CASE: WHEN, THEN, ELSE, and END. These additional keywords are needed to fully define the logic of the CASE expression. The WHEN and THEN keywords define a condition that is evaluated. If the value after the WHEN is true, then the result after THEN is utilized. The WHEN and THEN keywords can be repeated any number of times. When there is a WHEN, there must also be a corresponding THEN. The ELSE keyword is used to define a default value to be used if none of the WHEN-THEN conditions is true. As indicated by the brackets, the ELSE keyword is not required. However, it is generally a good idea to include the ELSE keyword in every CASE expression, so as to explicitly state a default value.

Let's look at a specific example, using this Products table:

ProductID	CategoryCode	ProductDescription
1	F	Apple
2	F	Orange
3	S	Mustard
4	V	Carrot

A SELECT with a CASE expression against data in this table might look like:

```
SELECT
CASE CategoryCode
WHEN 'F' THEN 'Fruit'
WHEN 'V' THEN 'Vegetable'
ELSE 'Other'
END AS 'Category',
ProductDescription AS 'Description'
FROM Products
```

and produces this output:

Category	Description
Fruit	Apple
Fruit	Orange
Other	Mustard
Vegetable	Carrot

Let's look at the previous SELECT statement line by line. The first line contains the SELECT keyword. The second line, with the CASE keyword, tells you that the CategoryCode column is to be analyzed. The third line introduces the first WHEN-THEN condition. This line says that if the CategoryCode column equals F, then the value to display should be "Fruit". The next line says that if it's V, then display "Vegetable". The ELSE line provides a default value of "Other" to use if the CategoryCode is not F or V. The END line terminates the CASE statement and also includes an AS keyword to provide a column alias for the CASE expression.

The next line with ProductDescription is merely another column and has nothing to do with the CASE expression.

The CASE expression is very useful for translating cryptic values into meaningful descriptions. In this example, the CategoryCode column in the Products table contains only a single character code to indicate the type of product. It's using F to denote Fruit, V for Vegetables, S for Spices, and so on. The CASE clause allows you to specify the translation.

The Searched Format

The general format for the searched CASE expression is:

```
CASE
WHEN condition1 THEN result1
WHEN condition2 THEN result2
repeat WHEN-THEN any number of times)
[ELSE DefaultResult]
END
```

The equivalent of the above SELECT statement using this second format is:

```
SELECT
CASE
WHEN CategoryCode = 'F' THEN 'Fruit'
WHEN CategoryCode = 'V' THEN 'Vegetable'
ELSE 'Other'
END AS 'Category',
ProductDescription AS 'Description'
FROM Products
```

The data retrieved is identical to the first format. Notice the subtle differences. In the simple format, the column name to be evaluated is placed after the CASE keyword, and the expression following the WHEN is a simple literal value. In the searched format, a column name to be evaluated is not put next to the CASE keyword. Instead, this format allows for a more complex conditional expression following the WHEN keyword.

For the previous example, either format of the CASE clause can be used, and it will produce the same result. Let's now look at another example for which only the searched format will yield the desired result.

This next example will be taken from this data:

ProductID	Fruit	Vegetable	Spice	ProductDescription
1	X			Apple
2	X			Orange
3			X	Mustard
4		X		Carrot

In this situation, the database contains multiple columns to indicate whether the product is a fruit, vegetable, or spice. A CASE expression to create the same output for this data is:

```
SELECT
CASE
WHEN Fruit = 'X' THEN 'Fruit'
WHEN Vegetable = 'X' THEN 'Vegetable'
ELSE 'Other'
END AS 'Category',
ProductDescription AS 'Description'
FROM Products
```

Once again, the result is:

Category	Description
Fruit	Apple
Fruit	Orange
Other	Mustard
Vegetable	Carrot

Since the data now uses three separate columns to indicate if the product is a fruit, vegetable, or spice, you need to use the searched format of the CASE clause in order to apply the needed logic. The simple format only works with an analysis of a single column.

Due to the inherent complexity of IF-THEN-ELSE logic, the CASE expression is one of the more challenging topics in this book. In this chapter, we have focused on using CASE expressions in the SELECT *columnlist*. However, CASE expressions can also be utilized in other SQL clauses, such as the ORDER BY clause, and other clauses not yet discussed, such as the WHERE and HAVING clauses.

Let's give just one example of additional uses of the CASE expression. Although we have not yet talked about the WHERE clause, let's imagine that we know something about it. As will be explained in Chapter 7, the WHERE clause allows you to apply selection criteria to the rows that will be presented to the user. A typical expression might be something like:

```
WHERE ProductDescription = 'White Glove'
```

This is a very specific directive. You only want to see rows where the product is a white glove. The value of the CASE expression is that it allows you to apply conditional logic to the value you're looking for, perhaps based on the value of some other column. For example, you may have another column, named ProductType, which gives more information about products. Using a CASE expression, you can select products that are white gloves if the ProductType equals X, or products that are socks if the ProductType equals Y. In essence, you can substitute a CASE expression for the value 'White Glove' in the WHERE clause in order to describe some more complex logic.

Looking Ahead

CASE expressions can be utilized to provide a logical evaluation for a column or expression in a SELECT *columnlist.* There are two basic formats for the expression: the simple and the searched. A typical use is to provide translations for data items with cryptic values. Finally, although this chapter is titled "Column-Based Logic," CASE expressions can be used in places other than the columns in a SELECT *columnlist.* They can be used anyplace where you would like to specify conditional logic for a specific column or data element.

In our next chapter, we are going to move beyond logic as it applies to column values and talk about how to apply logic to the selection of entire rows. This is the topic for which you've been patiently waiting, no doubt. The ability to specify selection criteria in your SELECT statements is critical to most normal queries. In the real world, it would be very unusual to issue a SELECT statement without some sort of selection criteria. The topics discussed in the next chapter will allow you to accomplish that objective.

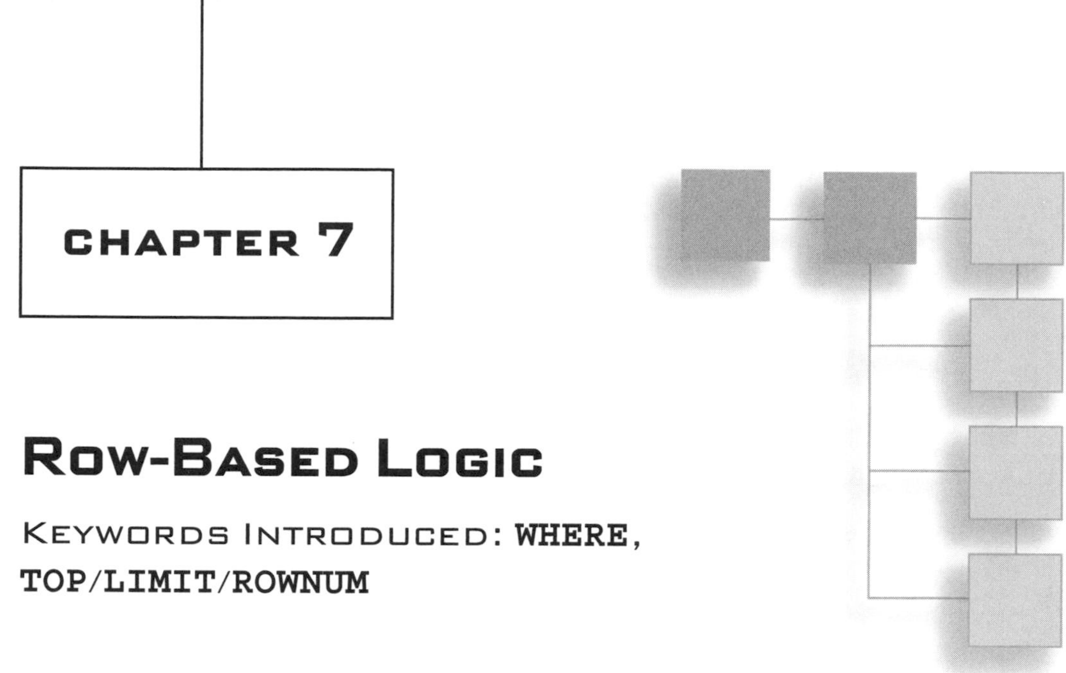

Chapter 7

Row-Based Logic

Keywords Introduced: **WHERE**, **TOP/LIMIT/ROWNUM**

At long last, I am now going to show you how to apply selection criteria to your tables. Up until this point, our SELECT statements have always brought back every row in the table. This would rarely be the case in real-world situations. Normally, you are interested in only retrieving data that meets certain criteria. The topics in this chapter will address this issue.

If you're selecting customers, then you would typically only get to see a subset of all your customers. If you're retrieving orders from your customers, you probably only want to see orders that meet certain conditions. If you're looking at products, then you're probably only interested in viewing certain types of products. Rarely does someone want to simply see everything. Your interest (or anyone else's) in your data is typically directed toward a small subset of data in order to analyze or view one particular aspect.

Applying Selection Criteria

Selection criteria in SQL begins with the WHERE clause. The WHERE keyword accomplishes the task of selecting a subset of rows. The logic utilized for the WHERE keyword builds on the column-based logic seen in the last chapter. The difference is that, whereas the CASE expression only allowed you to apply logic to a specific column, you are now going to apply logic to all the rows in a table.

This is the general format of the SELECT statement, including the WHERE clause and other clauses previously discussed:

```
SELECT columnlist
FROM tablelist
WHERE condition
ORDER BY columnlist
```

As can be seen, the WHERE clause must always be between the FROM and ORDER BY clauses. In fact, if any clause is used, it must appear in the order shown.

Let's look at an example, taken from data in this Orders table:

OrderID	FirstName	LastName	QuantityPurchased	PricePerItem
1	William	Smith	4	2.50
2	Natalie	Lopez	10	1.25
3	Brenda	Harper	5	4.00

We'll start with a statement with a simple WHERE clause:

```
SELECT
FirstName,
LastName,
QuantityPurchased
FROM Orders
WHERE LastName = 'Harper'
```

The output is:

FirstName	LastName	QuantityPurchased
Brenda	Harper	5

Since the WHERE clause stipulates to only select rows with a LastName equal to 'Harper', only one of the three rows in the table is returned.

Notice that the desired value of the LastName column was enclosed in quotes, due to the fact that LastName is a text column. For numeric fields, no quotes are necessary. For example, the following SELECT is equally valid and would have returned the same data:

```
SELECT
FirstName,
LastName,
QuantityPurchased
FROM Orders
WHERE QuantityPurchased = 5
```

WHERE Clause Operators

In the previous statements, an equals sign (=) is used as the operator in the `WHERE` clause. The equals sign indicates a test for equality. The general format shown above indicates that a *condition* follows the `WHERE` keyword. This condition consists of an operator with two expressions on either side.

The following is a list of the basic operators that can be used in the `WHERE` clause:

WHERE Operator	Meaning
=	equals
<>	does not equal
>	is greater than
<	is less than
>=	is greater than or equal to
<=	is less than or equal to

More advanced operators will be covered in the next chapter.

The meaning of the equals (=) and does not equal (<>) operators should be obvious. Here's an example of a `WHERE` clause with an "is greater than" operator, taken from the same Orders table:

```
SELECT
FirstName,
LastName,
QuantityPurchased
FROM Orders
WHERE QuantityPurchased > 6
```

The result is:

FirstName	LastName	QuantityPurchased
Natalie	Lopez	10

In this example, only one row meets the qualification that the QuantityPurchased column be greater than 6. Although not as commonly used, it's also possible to use the "is greater than" operator with a text column. This example:

```
SELECT
FirstName,
LastName
FROM Orders
WHERE LastName > 'K'
```

returns:

FirstName	LastName
William	Smith
Natalie	Lopez

Since the test is for last names greater than K, it only brings back Smith and Lopez, but not Harper. When applied to text fields, the greater than and less than operators indicate selection by the alphabetic order of the values. In this case, Smith and Lopez are returned, since S and L are after K in the alphabet.

Finally, it should be noted that all of these operators can also be used with the `WHEN` keyword in the searched format of the `CASE` expression. For example, a valid `CASE` expression might be:

```
CASE
WHEN column1 > value1 THEN result1
END
```

Limiting Rows

What do you do if you want to select a small subset of the rows in a table, but you don't care which rows are returned? Let's say that you have a table with 50,000 rows, and you want to see just a few rows of data to see what it looks like. It wouldn't make sense to use the `WHERE` clause for this purpose, since you don't care which rows are returned.

The solution is to use a special keyword to specify that you want to limit how many rows are returned. This is another instance where the syntax differs among databases. In Microsoft SQL Server, the keyword that accomplishes this task is `TOP`.

The general format is:

```
SELECT
TOP number
columnlist
FROM table
```

DATABASE DIFFERENCES: MySQL and Oracle

MySQL uses the keyword `LIMIT` rather than `TOP`. The general format is:

```
SELECT
columnlist
FROM table
LIMIT number
```

Oracle uses the keyword `ROWNUM` rather than `TOP`. The `ROWNUM` keyword needs to be specified in a `WHERE` clause, as follows:

```
SELECT
columnlist
FROM table
WHERE ROWNUM <- number
```

In the remainder of this chapter, you'll see statements using the Microsoft `TOP` keyword. If you're using MySQL or Oracle, you can simply substitute the equivalent `LIMIT` or `ROWNUM` keywords.

Let's say that you want to see the first 10 rows from a table. The `SELECT` to accomplish this looks like:

```
SELECT
TOP 10 *
FROM table
```

This statement returns all columns in the first 10 rows from the table. Like any `SELECT` statement without an `ORDER BY` clause, there's no way to predict which 10 rows will be returned. It depends on how the data is physically stored in the table.

Similarly, you can list specific columns to return:

```
SELECT
TOP 10
column1, column2
FROM table
```

In essence, the TOP keyword accomplishes something similar to the WHERE clause, because it permits you to return a small subset of rows in the specified table. Keep in mind, though, that rows returned using the TOP keyword are not a true random sample in a statistical sense. They're only the first rows that qualify, based on how the data is physically stored in the database.

Limiting Rows with a Sort

Another use of the TOP keyword is to use it in combination with the ORDER BY clause to obtain a certain number of rows with the highest values, based on a specified category. This type of data selection is commonly referred to as a *Top N* selection. Here's an example, taken from this Books table:

BookID	Title	Author	CurrentMonthSales
1	Pride and Prejudice	Austen	15
2	Animal Farm	Orwell	7
3	Merchant of Venice	Shakespeare	5
4	Romeo and Juliet	Shakespeare	8
5	Oliver Twist	Dickens	3
6	Candide	Voltaire	9
7	The Scarlet Letter	Hawthorne	12
8	Hamlet	Shakespeare	2

Let's say that you want to see the three books that sold the most in the current month. The SELECT to accomplish this is:

```
SELECT
TOP 3
Title AS 'Book Title',
CurrentMonthSales AS 'Quantity Sold'
FROM Books
ORDER BY CurrentMonthSales DESC
```

The output is:

Book Title	Quantity Sold
Pride and Prejudice	15
The Scarlet Letter	12
Candide	9

Let's examine this statement in some detail. The `TOP 3` in the second line indicates that only three rows are to be returned. The main question to ask is how it determines which three rows to display. The answer is found in the `ORDER BY` clause. If there were no `ORDER BY` clause, then `SELECT` would simply bring back any three rows of data, but that's not what you want. You're looking for the three rows with the highest sales. In order to accomplish this, you need to sort the rows by the CurrentMonthSales column in descending order. Why descending? Because when you sort in descending order, the highest numbers appear first. If you had sorted in ascending order, you would get the books with the least amount of sales, not the most.

Now, let's add one more twist to this scenario. Let's say that you only want to see the book by Shakespeare that sold the most. In order to accomplish this, you need to add a `WHERE` clausc, as follows:

```
SELECT
TOP 1
Title AS 'Book Title',
CurrentMonthSales AS 'Quantity Sold'
FROM Books
WHERE Author = 'Shakespeare'
ORDER BY CurrentMonthSales DESC
```

This brings back this data:

Book Title	Quantity Sold
Romeo and Juliet	8

The `WHERE` clause adds the qualification that you are only looking at books by Shakespeare. You also revised the `TOP` keyword to specify `TOP 1`, indicating that you only want to see one row of data.

DATABASE DIFFERENCES: Oracle

The procedure for limiting and sorting rows in Oracle is a bit more complex, since the ROWNUM is in the WHERE clause in Oracle syntax. You need to sort the data first and then apply the ROWNUM selection criteria. The general format is:

```
SELECT *
FROM
(SELECT
columnlist
FROM table
ORDER BY columnlist DESC)
WHERE ROWNUM <= number
```

This is an early example of a subquery, which will be covered in detail in Chapter 14. In brief, this statement consists of two separate SELECT statements. The inner SELECT, enclosed in parentheses, sorts the desired data by the specified *columnlist,* in descending order. The outer SELECT statement then retrieves data from the inner SELECT using the ROWNUM keyword to limit the number of rows that are displayed.

Looking Ahead

This chapter introduced the topic of how to apply selection criteria to queries. A number of basic operators, such as equals and greater than, were introduced. The ability to specify some basic selection criteria goes a long way towards making our SELECT statement truly useful. With the WHERE clause, you can now issue a statement that retrieves all customers from the state of New York.

The related topic of limiting the number of rows returned in a query was also covered in this chapter. Finally, the ability to limit rows in combination with an ORDER BY clause allows for a useful Top N type of data selection.

In our next chapter, "Boolean Logic," I am going to greatly enhance our selection criteria capabilities by introducing a bunch of new keywords that add sophisticated logic to the WHERE clause. Yes, it's true that you can now select customers from the state of New York, but what if you wanted to select customers who are in New York or California, but not in Buffalo or Los Angeles? The keywords covered in the next chapter will allow you to do that.

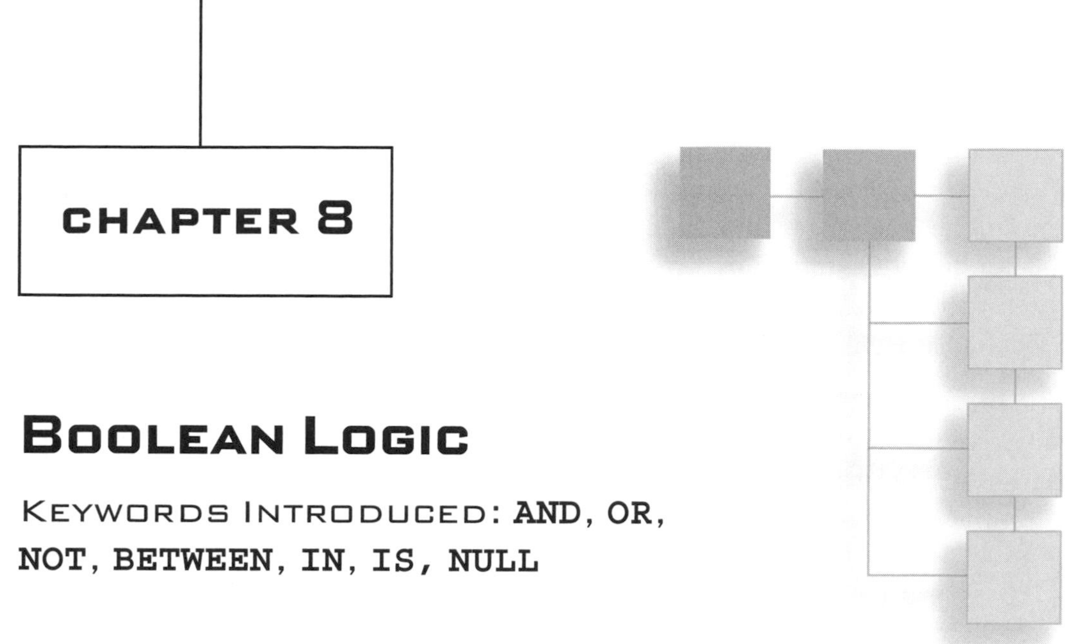

Chapter 8

Boolean Logic

Keywords Introduced: **AND**, **OR**, **NOT**, **BETWEEN**, **IN**, **IS**, **NULL**

In the previous chapter, we introduced the concept of selection criteria, but only in its simplest form. We're now going to expand on that concept to greatly enhance our ability to specify the rows that are returned from a SELECT. This is where the pure logic of SQL comes into play. In this chapter, we are going to introduce a number of operators that will allow you to create complex logical expressions.

With these new capabilities, if a user comes to you and says that she wants a list of all female customers who live in ZIP codes 60601 through 62999, but excluding anyone who's under the age of 30 or who doesn't have an email address, that will be something you can provide.

Complex Logical Conditions

The WHERE clause introduced in the previous chapter utilized only simple selection criteria. You saw WHERE clauses such as:

```
WHERE QuantityPurchased = 5
```

The condition expressed in this WHERE clause is quite simple: It returns all rows where the QuantityPurchased column has a value of 5.

In the real world, the selection of data is often far from straightforward. Accordingly, let's now turn our attention to ways of specifying some more complex logical conditions in your selection criteria.

The ability to devise complex logical conditions is sometimes called *Boolean logic.* This term, taken from mathematics, refers to the ability to formulate complex conditions that are evaluated as either true or false. In the aforementioned example, the condition QuantityPurchased = 5 is evaluated as either true or false for each row in the table. Obviously, you only want to see rows where the condition is evaluated as true.

The principle keywords used to create complex Boolean logic are `AND`, `OR`, and `NOT`. These three operators are used to add additional functionality to the `WHERE` clause. In the proper combination, the `AND`, `OR`, and `NOT` operators, along with parentheses, can specify just about any logical expression you can imagine.

The AND Operator

The following examples will all be taken from this Orders table:

OrderID	CustomerName	State	QuantityPurchased	PricePerItem
1	William Smith	IL	4	2.50
2	Natalie Lopez	CA	10	1.25
3	Brenda Harper	NY	5	4.00

Here's an example of a `WHERE` clause that uses the `AND` operator:

```
SELECT
CustomerName,
QuantityPurchased
FROM Orders
WHERE QuantityPurchased > 3
AND QuantityPurchased < 7
```

The `AND` clause means that all conditions must evaluate to true for the row to be selected.

This `SELECT` specifies that the only rows to be retrieved are those where the QuantityPurchased is both greater than 3 and less than 7. Therefore, only these two rows are returned:

CustomerName	QuantityPurchased
William Smith	4
Brenda Harper	5

Notice that the row for Natalie Lopez is not returned. Why? Natalie purchased a quantity of 10, which, in fact, does satisfy the first condition (QuantityPurchased > 3). However, the second condition (QuantityPurchased < 7) is not satisfied and therefore is not true. When using the AND operator, all conditions specified must be true.

The OR Operator

Let's now look at the OR operator. The AND clause meant that all conditions must evaluate to true for the row to be selected. The OR clause means that the row will be selected if *any* of the conditions is determined to be true.

Here's an example, taken from the same table:

```
SELECT
CustomerName,
QuantityPurchased,
PricePerItem
FROM Orders
WHERE QuantityPurchased > 8
OR PricePerItem > 3
```

The SELECT returns this data:

CustomerName	QuantityPurchased	PricePerItem
Natalie Lopez	10	1.25
Brenda Harper	5	4.00

Why are the rows for Natalie Lopez and Brenda Harper displayed, and not the row for William Smith? The row for Natalie Lopez is selected because it meets the requirements of the first condition (QuantityPurchased > 8). It doesn't matter that the second condition (PricePerItem > 3) isn't true, because only one condition needs to be true for an OR condition.

Likewise, the row for Brenda Harper is selected because the second condition (PricePerItem > 3) is true for that row. The row for William Smith isn't selected because it doesn't satisfy either of the two conditions.

Using Parentheses

Let's say that you are only interested in orders from customers from either the state of Illinois or the state of California. Additionally, you only want to see orders where the quantity purchased is greater than 8. To satisfy this request, you put together this SELECT statement:

```
SELECT
CustomerName,
State,
QuantityPurchased
FROM Orders
WHERE State = 'IL'
OR State = 'CA'
AND QuantityPurchased > 8
```

When you execute this, you are expecting to get back only one row, for Natalie Lopez. This is because you have two rows for customers in Illinois or California (Smith and Lopez). But only one of those (Lopez) has a quantity purchased greater than 8.

However, when you execute this statement, you see:

CustomerName	State	QuantityPurchased
William Smith	IL	4
Natalie Lopez	CA	10

What went wrong? Why did you get back two rows instead of one? The answer lies with how SQL interprets the WHERE clause, which contains both AND and OR operators. Like other computer languages, SQL has a predetermined order of evaluation, which specifies the order in which various operators are interpreted. Unless told otherwise, SQL always processes the AND operator before the OR operator. So, in the previous statement, it first looks at the AND and evaluates the condition:

```
State = 'CA'
AND QuantityPurchased > 8
```

The row that satisfies that condition is for Natalie Lopez. It then evaluates the OR operator, which allows for rows where the State equals IL. That adds in the row for William Smith. Therefore, it determines that both the William Smith and the Natalie Lopez rows meet the condition.

Obviously, this isn't what was meant. This type of problem often comes up when AND and OR operators are combined in a single WHERE clause. The way to resolve the ambiguity is to use parentheses to specify the exact order of evaluation that you would like. Anything in parentheses is always evaluated first.

Here's how parentheses can be added to the previous SELECT to correct the situation:

```
SELECT
CustomerName,
State,
QuantityPurchased
FROM Orders
WHERE (State = 'IL'
OR State = 'CA')
AND QuantityPurchased > 8
```

When this is executed, you now see this data:

CustomerName	State	QuantityPurchased
Natalie Lopez	CA	10

The parentheses in the SELECT statement force the OR expression (State = 'IL' OR State = 'CA') to be evaluated first. This produces the intended result.

Multiple Sets of Parentheses

Let's say that you want to select two different sets of rows from the Orders table: first, rows for customers in New York, and second, rows for customers in Illinois who have made a purchase with a quantity between 3 and 10. The following SELECT accomplishes this requirement:

```
SELECT
CustomerName,
State,
QuantityPurchased
FROM Orders
WHERE State = 'NY'
OR (State = 'IL'
AND (QuantityPurchased >= 3
AND QuantityPurchased <= 10))
```

The result is:

CustomerName	State	QuantityPurchased
William Smith	IL	4
Brenda Harper	NY	5

Notice there are two sets of parentheses in this statement. Our use of parentheses here is analogous to the parentheses used in the composite functions seen in Chapter 4. With regard to functions, if there is more than one set of parentheses, the innermost set of functions always gets evaluated first. The same is true of parentheses used in Boolean expressions. In this example, the innermost set of parentheses contains:

```
(QuantityPurchased >= 3
AND QuantityPurchased <= 10)
```

After this is evaluated for each row, you can then proceed outward to the second set of parentheses:

```
(State = 'IL'
AND (QuantityPurchased >= 3
AND QuantityPurchased <= 10))
```

Finally, you add in the final line in the `WHERE` clause (which is not enclosed in any parentheses at all):

```
WHERE State = 'NY'
OR (State = 'IL'
AND (QuantityPurchased >= 3
AND QuantityPurchased <= 10))
```

The NOT Operator

In addition to the `AND` and `OR` operators, it is often useful to use the `NOT` operator to express a complex logical condition. The `NOT` expresses a negation, or opposite, of whatever follows the `NOT`. Here's a simple example:

```
SELECT
CustomerName,
State,
```

```
QuantityPurchased
FROM Orders
WHERE NOT State = 'NY'
```

The result is:

CustomerName	State	QuantityPurchased
William Smith	IL	4
Natalie Lopez	CA	10

This specifies a selection of rows where the state is not equal to NY. In this simple case, the NOT operator is not truly necessary. The previous statement can also be accomplished via the following equivalent statement:

```
SELECT
CustomerName,
State,
QuantityPurchased
FROM Orders
WHERE State <> 'NY'
```

In this situation, the not equals operator (<>) accomplishes the same thing as the NOT operator.

Here's a more complex example with the NOT operator:

```
SELECT
CustomerName,
State,
QuantityPurchased
FROM Orders
WHERE NOT (State = 'IL'
OR State = 'NY')
```

The result is:

CustomerName	State	QuantityPurchased
Natalie Lopez	CA	10

When the NOT operator is used before a set of parentheses, it negates everything in the parentheses. In this example, you are looking for all rows where the state is *not* Illinois or New York.

Again, note that the NOT operator is not strictly necessary in this example. The previous query can also be accomplished via the following equivalent statement:

```
SELECT
CustomerName,
State,
QuantityPurchased
FROM Orders
WHERE State <> 'IL'
AND State <> 'NY'
```

You may need to think a minute about why the previous two statements are really equivalent. The first statement utilizes the NOT operator and a logical expression with an OR operator. The second statement converts the same logic into an expression with an AND operator.

Here's a final example of how the NOT operator can be used in a complex statement:

```
SELECT
CustomerName,
State,
QuantityPurchased
FROM Orders
WHERE NOT (State = 'IL'
AND QuantityPurchased > 3)
```

The result is:

CustomerName	State	QuantityPurchased
Natalie Lopez	CA	10
Brenda Harper	NY	5

As before, there is another way to express the previous statement without using the NOT:

```
SELECT
CustomerName,
State,
QuantityPurchased
FROM Orders
WHERE State <> 'IL'
OR QuantityPurchased <= 3
```

As seen in these examples, it may not be logically necessary to use the NOT operator in complex expressions with arithmetic operators such as equals (=) and less than (<). However, it's often more straightforward to place a NOT in front of a logical expression than to convert that expression to one that doesn't use the NOT. In other words, the NOT operator can provide a useful way of expressing your logical thoughts.

The BETWEEN Operator

We will now turn to two special operators that can simplify expressions that would ordinarily require the OR or AND operators. These are the BETWEEN and IN operators. The BETWEEN operator allows you to abbreviate an AND expression with greater than or equal to (>=) and less than or equal to (<=) operators into one simple expression with a single operator.

Here's an example. Let's say you want to select all rows with a quantity purchased between 5 and 20. You can issue the following SELECT statement:

```
SELECT
CustomerName,
QuantityPurchased
FROM Orders
WHERE QuantityPurchased >= 5
AND QuantityPurchased <= 20
```

or you can issue this equivalent statement that utilizes the BETWEEN operator:

```
SELECT
CustomerName,
QuantityPurchased
FROM Orders
WHERE QuantityPurchased BETWEEN 5 AND 20
```

In both cases, the SELECT returns this data:

CustomerName	QuantityPurchased
Natalie Lopez	10
Brenda Harper	5

The BETWEEN operator always requires a corresponding AND placed between the two numbers.

Note the relative simplicity of the BETWEEN operator. Also notice that the BETWEEN keyword is equivalent only to the greater than or equal to (>=) and less than or equal to (<=) operators. It can't be used to express something simply greater than (>) or less than (<) a range of numbers. In this example, the row for Brenda Harper is selected since the quantity is equal to 5, and therefore is between 5 and 20.

The NOT operator can be used with the BETWEEN. For example, this SELECT:

```
SELECT
CustomerName,
QuantityPurchased
FROM Orders
WHERE QuantityPurchased NOT BETWEEN 5 AND 20
```

retrieves this data:

CustomerName	QuantityPurchased
William Smith	4

The IN Operator

Just as the BETWEEN represents a special case of the AND operator, the IN operator allows for a special case of the OR. Let's say you want to see rows where the state is Illinois or New York. You can issue this SELECT statement:

```
SELECT
CustomerName,
State
FROM Orders
WHERE State = 'IL'
OR State = 'NY'
```

or you can use this equivalent statement that utilizes the `IN` operator:

```
SELECT
CustomerName,
State
FROM Orders
WHERE State IN ('IL', 'NY')
```

In either case, the data retrieved is:

CustomerName	State
William Smith	IL
Brenda Harper	NY

Notice that commas are used to separate all values within the parentheses following the `IN` keyword.

The usefulness of the `IN` operator may not be obvious in this example, where only two states are listed. However, the `IN` can just as easily be used in situations where you want to list dozens of specific values. This greatly reduces the amount of typing required for such a statement. Another handy use for the IN operator comes in situations where you want to use data from Excel in a SQL statement. If you want to obtain multiple values from adjacent cells in a spreadsheet for your SQL statement, Excel allows you to copy those values with a comma delimiter. This result can then be pasted inside the parentheses following the `IN` operator.

As with the `BETWEEN` operator, the `NOT` operator can be used with the `IN`, as shown in this example:

```
SELECT
CustomerName,
State
FROM Orders
WHERE State NOT IN ('IL', 'NY')
```

This retrieves this data:

CustomerName	State
Natalie Lopez	CA

One final note about the IN operator. There is a second way to use the IN, which is substantially different from the syntax just discussed. In the second format of the IN operator, an entire SELECT statement is specified within the parentheses, allowing the individual values to be created logically when needed. This is called a *subquery,* and it will be covered in detail in Chapter 14.

Boolean Logic and NULL Values

At the start of this chapter, I stated that the Boolean logic in SQL evaluates complex expressions as either true or false. This assertion was not completely correct. When evaluating the conditions in a WHERE clause, there are actually three possibilities: true, false, and unknown. The possibility of unknown derives from the fact that columns in SQL databases are sometimes allowed to have a NULL value. As mentioned in Chapter 1, NULL values are those for which there is an absence of data.

SQL provides a special keyword to test for the presence of NULL values for a column specified in a WHERE clause. The keyword is IS NULL. Let's look at an example taken from the following Products table:

ProductID	ProductDescription	Weight
1	Printer A	NULL
2	Printer B	0
3	Monitor C	2
4	Laptop D	4

For this example, you have to imagine that as rows are added to the Products table, they are initially not given any value in the Weight column. They are initially given a value of NULL, and a user of the system later assigns a weight to the product.

Let's say that you attempt to use the following SELECT to find products missing a weight:

```
SELECT
ProductDescription,
Weight
FROM Products
WHERE Weight = 0
```

This would return:

ProductDescription	Weight
Printer B	0

This is not quite what you want. A weight equal to zero is not the same as a weight with a NULL value. To correct this, you need to issue:

```
SELECT
ProductDescription,
Weight
FROM Products
WHERE Weight = 0
OR Weight IS NULL
```

This returns:

ProductDescription	Weight
Printer A	NULL
Printer B	0

The `IS NULL` keyword can also be negated as `IS NOT NULL`, which allows you to retrieve all rows that do not have NULL for the specified column.

It should be mentioned that the `ISNULL` function, discussed in Chapter 4, can provide an alternative to the `IS NULL` keyword. The equivalent of the previous `SELECT` statement, utilizing the `ISNULL` function is:

```
SELECT
ProductDescription,
Weight
FROM Products
WHERE ISNULL(Weight, 0) = 0
```

This `SELECT` retrieves the same two rows. The `ISNULL` function converts all values for the Weight column with a value of NULL to 0. Since the `WHERE` clauses tests for a value of 0, it, in effect, tests for values of 0 or NULL.

You can also combine the ISNULL function and the IS NULL keyword in a single SELECT statement, such as:

```
SELECT
ProductDescription,
ISNULL (Weight, 0) AS 'Weight'
FROM Products
WHERE Weight = 0
OR Weight IS NULL
```

This produces this data:

ProductDescription	Weight
Printer A	0
Printer B	0

Looking Ahead

This chapter covered the important topic of how to create complex expressions of selection logic. The basic Boolean operators used in this endeavor were AND, OR, and NOT. We also discussed the BETWEEN and IN operators, which allow for a more concise statement of the AND and OR operators in certain situations. Parentheses are another essential tool in the formulation of complex expressions. By using parentheses or multiple sets of parentheses, you can create almost every imaginable logical condition. Finally, we talked about how to deal with NULL values when selecting data.

In our next chapter, we're going to take an interesting detour into some alternative ways to specify selection criteria. We're first going to look at the topic of pattern matching. This will allow you to match by portions of a word or phrase and to do such things as find all products that contain the word "white." The second half of the chapter will turn to the possibility of matching by the sound of a word or phrase. This, for example, will let you find all customers who have a first name that sounds like Haley, even if the name is spelled Hailey.

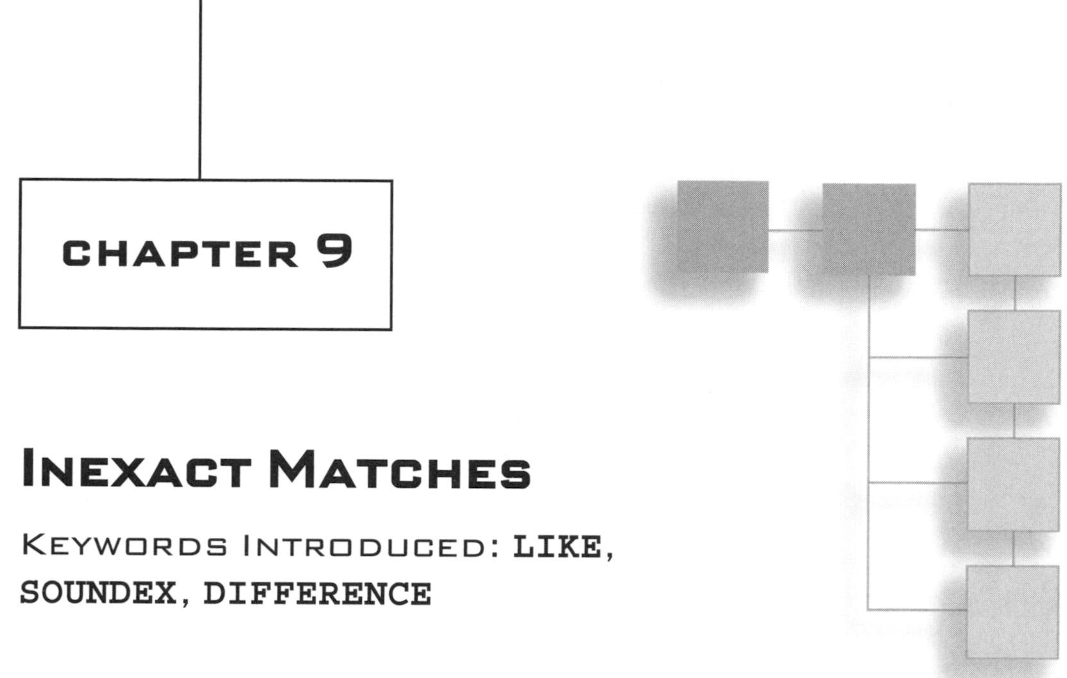

CHAPTER 9

Inexact Matches

Keywords Introduced: **LIKE**, **SOUNDEX**, **DIFFERENCE**

I would like to now turn to two situations in which the data to be retrieved is not precisely defined. In the first circumstance, we will look at the need to retrieve data based on inexact matches with words or phrases. For example, you may be interested in finding customers whose name contains the word "bank."

In the second situation, we will extend the idea of inexact matches to include the possibility of matching by the sound of a word or phrase. For instance, you may be interested in customers whose name sounds like "Smith," even though it may not be spelled exactly that way.

Pattern Matching

Let's first look at inexact matches within phrases, which is often referred to as *pattern matching*. In SQL, the `LIKE` operator is utilized in the `WHERE` clause to enable you to find matches against parts of a column value. The `LIKE` operator requires the use of special wildcard characters to specify exactly how the match is to work. Let's start with an example from the Movies table shown on the next page.

Our first example of a `SELECT` statement with a `LIKE` operator is:

```
SELECT
MovieTitle AS 'Movie'
FROM Movies
WHERE MovieTitle LIKE '%LOVE%'
```

MovieID	MovieTitle
1	Love Actually
2	His Girl Friday
3	Love and Death
4	Sweet and Lowdown
5	Everyone Says I Love You
6	Down with Love
7	101 Dalmatians

In this example, the percent (%) symbol is used as a wildcard. The percent (%) wildcard means *any characters.* It can also represent a list of zero characters. The percent (%) before LOVE means that you will accept a phrase with any characters before LOVE. Similarly, the percent (%) after LOVE means that you will accept a phrase with any characters after LOVE.

DATABASE DIFFERENCES: Oracle

Unlike Microsoft SQL Server and MySQL, Oracle is case sensitive when determining matches for literal values. In Oracle, LOVE is not the same as Love. An equivalent statement in Oracle is:

```
SELECT
MovieTitle AS Movie
FROM Movies
WHERE MovieTitle LIKE '%Love%';
```

A better solution in Oracle is to use the `UPPER` function to convert your data to uppercase, as follows:

```
SELECT
MovieTitle AS Movie
FROM Movies
WHERE UPPER (MovieTitle) LIKE '%LOVE%';
```

In other words, you are looking for any movie title that contains the phrase LOVE. Here is the data returned from the previous `SELECT`:

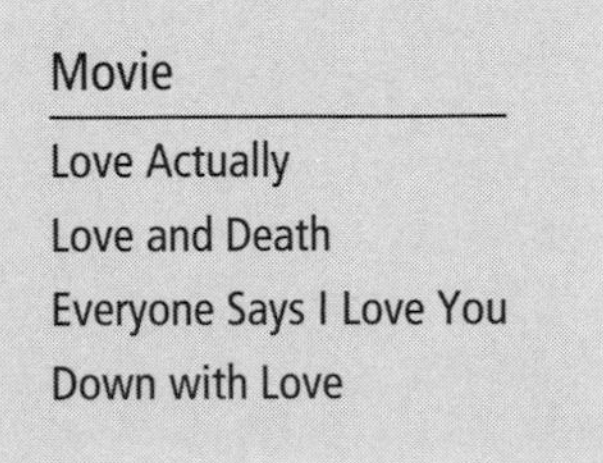

Movie
Love Actually
Love and Death
Everyone Says I Love You
Down with Love

Notice that LOVE appears as the first word, the last word, and sometimes in the middle of the movie title.

Let's now attempt to find only movies that begin with LOVE. If you issue:

```
SELECT
MovieTitle AS 'Movie'
FROM Movies
WHERE MovieTitle LIKE 'LOVE%'
```

you will only retrieve this data:

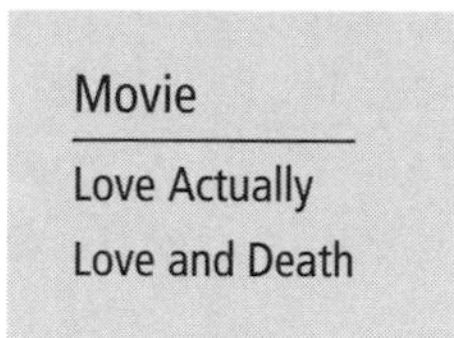

Movie
Love Actually
Love and Death

Since you are now specifying the percent (%) wildcard after the phrase LOVE, you will only get back movies that begin with LOVE.

Similarly, if you issue:

```
SELECT
MovieTitle AS 'Movie'
FROM Movies
WHERE MovieTitle LIKE '%LOVE'
```

you only get this data:

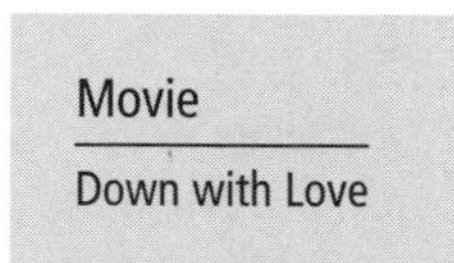

Movie
Down with Love

This is because you now specified that the phrase must *end* with the phrase LOVE.

What if you only want to see movies that contain the word LOVE in the middle of the title, but you don't want to see movies where it is at the beginning or end? The solution is to specify:

```
SELECT
MovieTitle AS 'Movie'
FROM Movies
WHERE MovieTitle LIKE '% LOVE %'
```

Notice that a space has been inserted between the phrase LOVE and the percent (%) wildcards on either side. This ensures that there is at least one space on either side of the word. The data brought back from this statement is:

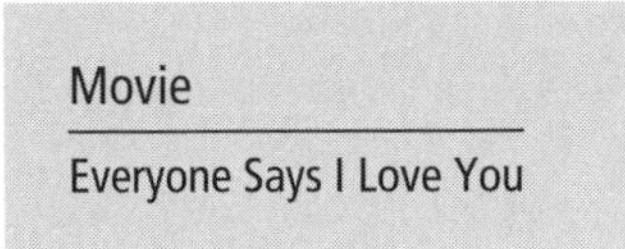

Movie
Everyone Says I Love You

Wildcards

The percent (%) symbol is the most common wildcard used with the `LIKE` operator. However, there are a few other possibilities. These include the underscore character (_), a *characterlist* enclosed in square brackets, and a caret symbol (^) plus a *characterlist* enclosed in square brackets. The following table lists these wildcards and their meanings:

Wildcard	Meaning
%	any characters (can be zero characters)
_	exactly one character (can be any character)
[*characterlist*]	exactly one character in the character list
[^*characterlist*]	exactly one character not in the character set

We're going to use the following Actors table to illustrate statements for the remainder of this chapter:

ActorID	FirstName	LastName
1	Cary	Grant
2	Mary	Steenburgen
3	Jon	Voight
4	Dustin	Hoffman
5	John	Wayne
6	Gary	Cooper
7	Julie	Andrews

Here's an illustration of how the underscore (_) wildcard character can be used:

```
SELECT
FirstName,
LastName
FROM Actors
WHERE FirstName LIKE '_ARY'
```

The output of this `SELECT` is:

FirstName	LastName
Cary	Grant
Mary	Steenburgen
Gary	Cooper

This statement retrieves these three actors because all have a first name consisting of exactly one character, followed by the phrase ARY.

Likewise, if you issue this statement:

```
SELECT
FirstName,
LastName
FROM Actors
WHERE FirstName LIKE 'J_N'
```

it produces:

FirstName	LastName
Jon	Voight

The actor John Wayne is not selected since John doesn't fit the J_N pattern. An underscore can only stand for one character.

The final wildcards we'll discuss, [*characterlist*] and [^*characterlist*], enable you to specify multiple wildcard values in a single position.

DATABASE DIFFERENCES: MySQL and Oracle

The [*characterlist*] and [^*characterlist*] wildcards are not available in MySQL or Oracle.

The following illustrates the [*characterlist*] wildcard:

```
SELECT
FirstName,
LastName
FROM Actors
WHERE FirstName LIKE '[CM]ARY'
```

This retrieves any rows where FirstName begins with a C or M and ends with ARY. The result is:

FirstName	LastName
Cary	Grant
Mary	Steenburgen

The following illustrates the [^*characterlist*] wildcard:

```
SELECT
FirstName,
LastName
FROM Actors
WHERE FirstName LIKE '[^CG]ARY'
```

This selects any rows where FirstName does *not* begin with a C or G and ends with ARY. The result is:

FirstName	LastName
Mary	Steenburgen

Finally, it should be noted that the `NOT` operator can be combined with `LIKE`, as in this example:

```
SELECT
FirstName,
LastName
FROM Actors
WHERE FirstName LIKE '%ARY%'
AND FirstName NOT LIKE '[MG]ARY'
```

The result is:

FirstName	LastName
Cary	Grant

Matching by Sound

Let's turn from matching letters and characters to matching sounds. SQL provides two functions that give you some interesting ways to compare the sounds of words or phrases. The two functions are SOUNDEX and DIFFERENCE.

Let's first look at an example that utilizes the SOUNDEX function:

```
SELECT
SOUNDEX ('Smith') AS 'Sound of Smith',
SOUNDEX ('Smythe') AS 'Sound of Smythe'
```

The result is:

Sound of Smith	Sound of Smythe
S530	S530

The SOUNDEX function always returns a four-character response, which is a sort of code for the sound of the phrase. The first character is always the first letter of the phrase. In this case, the first character is S because both Smith and Smythe begin with an S.

The remaining three characters are calculated from an analysis of the sound of the rest of the phrase. Internally, the function first removes all vowels and the letter Y. So, the function takes the MITH from SMITH and converts it to MTH. Likewise, it takes the MYTHE from SMYTHE and converts it to MTH. It then assigns a number to represent the sound of the phrase. In this example, that number turns out to be 530.

Since SOUNDEX returns a value of S530 for both Smith and Smythe, you can conclude that they probably have very similar sounds.

Microsoft SQL Server provides one additional function, called DIFFERENCE, which works in conjunction with the SOUNDEX function.

DATABASE DIFFERENCES: MySQL and Oracle

The `DIFFERENCE` function isn't available in MySQL or Oracle.

Here's an example, using the same words:

```
SELECT
DIFFERENCE ('Smith', 'Smythe') AS 'The Difference'
```

The result is:

The Difference
4

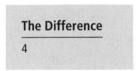

The `DIFFERENCE` function always requires two arguments. Internally, the function first retrieves the `SOUNDEX` values for each of the arguments and then compares those values. If it returns a value of 4, as in the previous example, that means that all four characters in the `SOUNDEX` value are identical. A value of 0 means that none of the characters is identical. Therefore, a `DIFFERENCE` value of 4 indicates the highest possible match, and a value of 0 is the lowest possible match.

With this in mind, here's an example of how the `DIFFERENCE` function can be used to retrieve values that are very similar in sound to a specific phrase. Working from the Actors table, you're going to attempt to find rows with a first name that sounds like John. The `SELECT` statement is:

```
SELECT
FirstName,
LastName
FROM Actors
WHERE DIFFERENCE (FirstName, 'John') = 4
```

The results are:

FirstName	LastName
Jon	Voight
John	Wayne

The DIFFERENCE function concluded that both John and Jon had a difference value of 4 between the name and the specified value of John.

If you want to analyze exactly why these two rows were selected, you can alter your SELECT to show both the SOUNDEX and DIFFERENCE values for all rows in the table:

```
SELECT
FirstName,
LastName,
DIFFERENCE (FirstName, 'John') AS 'Difference Value',
SOUNDEX (FirstName) AS 'Soundex Value'
FROM Actors
```

This returns:

FirstName	LastName	Difference Value	Soundex Value
Cary	Grant	2	C600
Mary	Steenburgen	2	M600
Jon	Voight	4	J500
Dustin	Hoffman	1	D235
John	Wayne	4	J500
Gary	Cooper	2	G600
Julie	Andrews	3	J400

Notice that both Jon Voight and John Wayne have a SOUNDEX value of J500 and a DIFFERENCE value of 4 for their first names. This explains why they were initially selected. Also notice that Julie Andrews has a DIFFERENCE value of 3. If you had specified a WHERE clause where the DIFFERENCE value equaled 3 or 4, that actor would have been selected as well.

Looking Ahead

This concludes our study of matching phrases by pattern or sound. Matching by patterns is an important and widely used function of SQL. Any time you enter a word in a search box and attempt to retrieve all entities containing that word, you are utilizing pattern matching. Efforts to match by sound are much less common. The technology exists, but there is an inherent difficulty in translating words to sounds. The English language, or any language for that matter, contains too many quirks and exceptions for such a match to be reliable.

In our next chapter, "Summarizing Data," we're going to turn our attention to ways to separate data into groups and summarize the values in those groups with various statistics. Back in Chapter 4, we talked about scalar functions. The next chapter will introduce another type of function, called *aggregate functions.* These aggregate functions will allow you to summarize your data in many useful ways. For example, you'll be able to look at any group of orders and determine the number of orders, the total dollar amount of the orders, and the average order size. With these techniques, you'll be able to move beyond the presentation of detailed data and begin to truly add value for your users as you deliver summarized information.

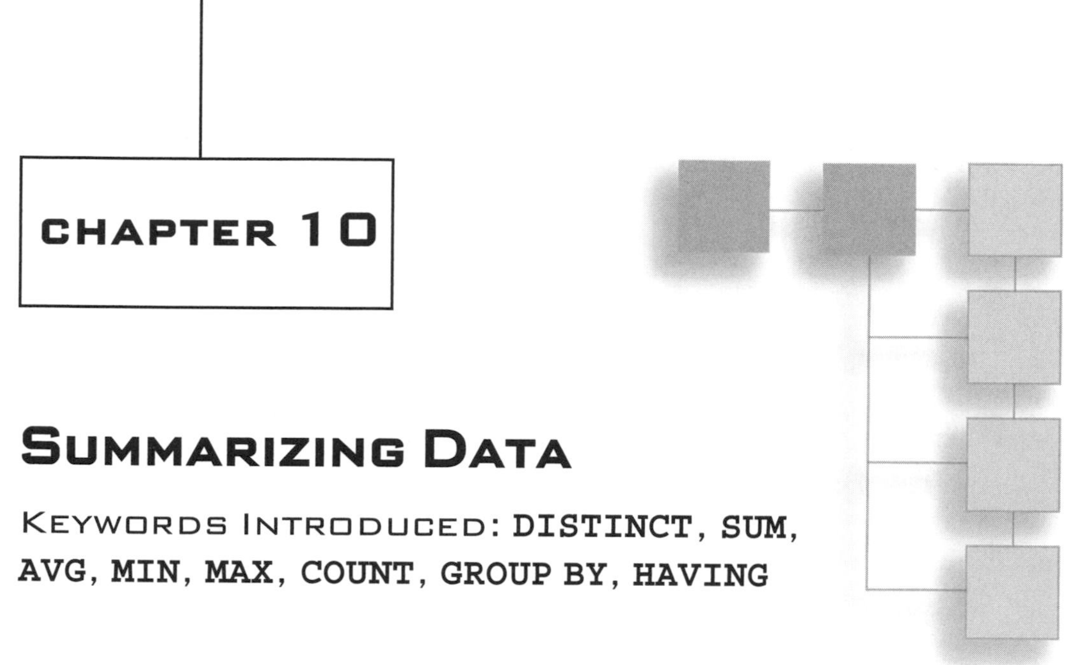

Chapter 10

Summarizing Data

Keywords Introduced: DISTINCT, SUM, AVG, MIN, MAX, COUNT, GROUP BY, HAVING

Up until now, we've been presenting data basically as it exists in a database. Sure, we've used some functions to move things around and have created some additional calculations, but the rows we've retrieved have corresponded to rows in the underlying database. We now want to turn to various methods to summarize our data.

The computer term usually associated with this type of endeavor is *aggregation,* which means "to combine into groups." The ability to aggregate and summarize your data is key to being able to move beyond a mere display of data to something approaching real information. There's a bit of magic involved when users view summarized data in a report. They understand and appreciate that you've been able to extract some real meaning from the mass of data in a database, in order to present a clearer picture of what it all means.

Eliminating Duplicates

Although it doesn't provide a true aggregation, the most elementary way to summarize data is to eliminate duplicates. SQL has a keyword named DISTINCT, which provides an easy way to remove duplicate rows from your output.

Here's an example of the DISTINCT keyword, used with the following SongTitles table:

SongID	Artist	Album	Title
1	The Beatles	Abbey Road	Come Together
2	The Beatles	Abbey Road	Sun King
3	The Beatles	Revolver	Yellow Submarine
4	The Rolling Stones	Let It Bleed	Monkey Man
5	The Rolling Stones	Flowers	Ruby Tuesday
6	Paul McCartney	Ram	Smile Away

Let's say you want to see a list of artists in the table. This can be accomplished with:

```
SELECT
DISTINCT
Artist
FROM SongTitles
ORDER BY Artist
```

The results are:

Artist
Paul McCartney
The Beatles
The Rolling Stones

The DISTINCT keyword is always placed immediately after the SELECT keyword. The DISTINCT specifies that only unique values of the *columnlist* that follow are to be brought back. In this case, there are only three unique artists, so only three rows are returned.

If you want to see unique combinations of both artists and albums, you'd issue:

```
SELECT
DISTINCT
Artist,
```

```
Album
FROM SongTitles
ORDER BY Artist, Album
```

and the results would be:

Artist	Album
Paul McCartney	Ram
The Beatles	Abbey Road
The Beatles	Revolver
The Rolling Stones	Flowers
The Rolling Stones	Let It Bleed

Notice that Abbey Road is only listed once, even though there are two songs from that album in the table. This is because the DISTINCT keyword causes only unique values from the listed columns to be shown.

Aggregate Functions

The functions we discussed in Chapter 4 were all *scalar functions*. These functions were all performed on a single number or value. In contrast, *aggregate functions* are meant to be used with groups of data. The mostly widely used aggregate functions are COUNT, SUM, AVG, MIN, and MAX. These provide counts, sums, averages, and minimum and maximum values of groups of data.

All of our aggregate function examples will be taken from the following two tables with data about students, fees, and grades. The Fees table contains:

FeeID	Student	FeeType	Fee
1	George	Gym	30
2	George	Lunch	10
3	George	Trip	8
4	Janet	Gym	30
5	Alan	Lunch	10

Here's the Grades table:

GradeID	Student	GradeType	Grade
1	Susan	Quiz	92
2	Susan	Quiz	95
3	Susan	Homework	84
4	Kathy	Quiz	62
5	Kathy	Quiz	81
6	Kathy	Homework	NULL
7	Alec	Quiz	58
8	Alec	Quiz	74
9	Alec	Homework	88

Starting with the SUM function, let's say that you want to see the total amount of gym fees paid by all students. This can be accomplished with:

```
SELECT
SUM (Fee) AS 'Total Gym Fees'
FROM Fees
WHERE FeeType = 'Gym'
```

The resulting data is:

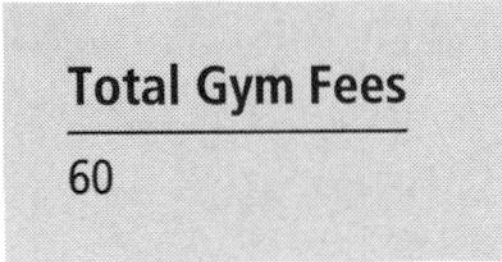

Total Gym Fees
60

As can be seen, the SUM function sums up the total values for the Fee column, subject to selection in the WHERE clause. Since the only expression in the *columnlist* is an aggregate function, the query returns only one row of data, giving the aggregate amount.

DATABASE DIFFERENCES: MySQL

As noted in Chapter 4, MySQL sometimes requires that there be no space between a function name and the left parenthesis. This is also true of most aggregate functions. For example, the previous statement needs to be written as the following in MySQL:

```
SELECT
SUM(Fee) AS 'Total Gym Fees'
```

```
FROM Fees
WHERE FeeType = 'Gym'
```

The AVG, MIN, and MAX functions are quite similar. Here's an example of the AVG function. In this case, we're seeking to obtain the average grade of all quizzes in the Grades table:

```
SELECT
AVG (Grade) AS 'Average Quiz Score'
FROM Grades
WHERE GradeType = 'Quiz'
```

The result is:

Average Quiz Score
77

More than one aggregate function can be used in a single SELECT statement. Here's a SELECT that illustrates AVG, MIN, and MAX in a single statement:

```
SELECT
AVG (Grade) AS 'Average Quiz Score',
MIN (Grade) AS 'Minimum Quiz Score',
MAX (Grade) AS 'Maximum Quiz Score'
FROM Grades
WHERE GradeType = 'Quiz'
```

The result is:

Average Quiz Score	Minimum Quiz Score	Maximum Quiz Score
77	58	95

The numbers you see have been computed separately. The output shows the average, minimum, and maximum of all quizzes in the Grades table.

The COUNT Function

The COUNT function is slightly more complex, in that it can be used in three different ways.

First, the COUNT function can be used to return a count of all selected rows, regardless of the values in any particular column. As an example, the following returns a count of all rows with homework grades:

```
SELECT
COUNT (*) AS 'Count of Homework Rows'
FROM Grades
WHERE GradeType = 'Homework'
```

The result is:

Count of Homework Rows
3

The asterisk in the parentheses means "all columns." SQL retrieves all columns in those rows that are selected, and then it returns a count of the number of rows.

In the second format of the COUNT function, a specific column is specified rather than the asterisk. Here's an example:

```
SELECT
COUNT (Grade) AS 'Count of Homework Scores'
FROM Grades
WHERE GradeType = 'Homework'
```

The result is:

Count of Homework Scores
2

Notice the subtle difference between the previous two SELECT statements. In the first, you're merely counting rows where the GradeType equals "Homework." There are three of these rows. In the second, you're counting occurrences of the Grade column where the GradeType column has a value of "Homework." In this case, one of the three rows has a value of NULL in the Grade column, so it isn't counted. As you remember, NULL means that the data doesn't exist.

The third format of the COUNT function allows you to use the DISTINCT keyword in addition to a column name. Here's an example:

```
SELECT
COUNT (DISTINCT FeeType) AS 'Number of Fee Types'
FROM Fees
```

This statement is counting the number of distinct values for the FeeType column. The result is:

Number of Fee Types
3

This means that there are three different values found in the FeeType column.

Grouping Data

The previous examples of aggregation functions are interesting, but of somewhat limited value. The real power of the aggregation functions will become evident after we introduce the concept of grouping data.

The GROUP BY keyword is used to separate data returned from a SELECT statement into any number of groups. For example, when looking at the previous Grades table, you may be interested in analyzing test scores based on the grade type. In other words, you want to separate the data into two separate groups, quizzes and homework. The value of the GradeType column can be used to determine which group each row belongs to.

Once data has been separated into groups, then aggregation functions can be utilized so that summary statistics for each of the groups can be calculated and compared.

Let's proceed with an example that introduces the GROUP BY keyword:

```
SELECT
GradeType AS 'Grade Type',
AVG (Grade) AS 'Average Grade'
FROM Grades
GROUP BY GradeType
ORDER BY GradeType
```

The result is:

Grade Type	Average Grade
Homework	86
Quiz	77

In this example, the GROUP BY keyword specifies that groups are to be created based on the value of the GradeType column. The two columns in the SELECT *columnlist* are GradeType and a calculated field that uses the AVG function. The GradeType column was included in the *columnlist* because when creating a group, it's usually a good idea to include the column on which the groups are based. The "Average Grade" calculated field aggregates values based on all rows in each group.

Notice that the average homework grade has been computed as 86. Even though there is one row with a NULL value for the Homework type, SQL is smart enough to ignore rows with NULL values when computing an average. If you want the NULL value to be counted as a 0, then the ISNULL function can used to convert the NULL to a 0, as follows:

```
AVG (ISNULL (Grade, 0)) AS 'Average Grade'
```

It's important to note that when using a GROUP BY keyword, all columns in the *columnlist* must either be listed as columns in the GROUP BY clause or else be used in an aggregation function. Nothing else would make any sense. For example, the following SELECT would error:

```
SELECT
GradeType AS 'Grade Type',
AVG (Grade) AS 'Average Grade',
Student AS 'Student'
FROM Grades
GROUP BY GradeType
ORDER BY GradeType
```

The problem with this statement is that the Student column is not in the GROUP BY clause, nor is it aggregated in any way. Since everything is being presented in groups, SQL doesn't know what to do with the Student column.

DATABASE DIFFERENCES: MySQL

Unlike Microsoft SQL Server and Oracle, the previous statement will not error in MySQL, but will produce incorrect results.

Multiple Columns and Sorting

The concept of groups can be extended so the groups are based on more than one column. Let's go back to the last SELECT and add the Student column to the GROUP BY clause and also to the *columnlist*. It now looks like:

```
SELECT
GradeType AS 'Grade Type',
Student AS 'Student',
AVG (Grade) AS 'Average Grade'
FROM Grades
GROUP BY GradeType, Student
ORDER BY GradeType, Student
```

The resulting data is:

Grade Type	Student	Average Grade
Homework	Alec	88
Homework	Kathy	NULL
Homework	Susan	84
Quiz	Alec	66
Quiz	Kathy	71.5
Quiz	Susan	93.5

You now see a breakdown not only of grade types, but also of students. The average grades are computed on each group. Note that the Homework row for Kathy shows a NULL value, since she only has one homework row, and that row has a value of NULL for the grade.

The order in which columns are listed in the GROUP BY clause has no significance. The results would be the same if the clause were:

```
GROUP BY Student, GradeType
```

However, as always, the order that columns are listed in the ORDER BY clause is meaningful. If you switch the ORDER BY clause to:

```
ORDER BY Student, GradeType
```

then the results are:

Grade Type	Student	Average
Homework	Alec	88
Quiz	Alec	66
Homework	Kathy	NULL
Quiz	Kathy	71.5
Homework	Susan	84
Quiz	Susan	93.5

This still looks a bit strange, since it's difficult to tell at a glance that the data is really sorted by Student and then by Grade Type. As a general rule of thumb, it often helps if columns are listed in the same order in which columns are sorted. A more understandable SELECT statement would be:

```
SELECT
Student AS 'Student',
GradeType AS 'Grade Type',
AVG (Grade) AS 'Average Grade'
FROM Grades
GROUP BY GradeType, Student
ORDER BY Student, GradeType
```

The data now looks like:

Student	Grade Type	Average Grade
Alec	Homework	88
Alec	Quiz	66
Kathy	Homework	NULL
Kathy	Quiz	71.5
Susan	Homework	84
Susan	Quiz	93.5

This is more comprehensible, since the column order corresponds to the sort order.

There's sometimes a certain confusion as to the difference between the GROUP BY and ORDER BY clauses. Just remember that the GROUP BY merely creates the groups. You still need to use the ORDER BY to present your data in the correct sequence.

Selection Criteria on Aggregates

One more topic needs to be added to our discussion of summarizing data. Once groups are created, selection criteria becomes a bit more complex. When applying any kind of selection criteria to a SELECT with a GROUP BY, one has to ask whether the selection criteria applies to the individual rows or to the entire group.

In essence, the WHERE clause handles selection criteria for individual rows. SQL provides a keyword named HAVING, which allows for selection criteria at the group level.

Returning to the Grades table, let's say you want to only look at grades on quizzes that are 70 or higher. The grades you'd like to look at are individual grades, so you can use the WHERE clause, as normal. Such a SELECT might look like:

```
SELECT
Student AS 'Student',
GradeType AS 'Grade Type',
Grade AS 'Grade'
FROM Grades
WHERE GradeType = 'Quiz'
AND Grade >= 70
ORDER BY Student, Grade
```

The resulting data is:

Student	GradeType	Grade
Alec	Quiz	74
Kathy	Quiz	81
Susan	Quiz	92
Susan	Quiz	95

Notice that quizzes with a score less than 70 aren't shown. For example, you can see Alec's quiz score of 74, but not his quiz score of 58.

But what if you want to only display data for students who have an *average* quiz grade of 70 or more? Then you want to select on an average, not on individual rows. This is where the HAVING keyword comes in. You need to first group grades by student and then apply your selection criteria to an aggregate statistic based on the entire group. The following statement produces what we desire:

```
SELECT
Student AS 'Student',
AVG (Grade) AS 'Average Quiz Grade'
FROM Grades
WHERE GradeType = 'Quiz'
GROUP BY Student
HAVING AVG (Grade) >= 70
ORDER BY Student
```

The output is:

Student	Average Quiz Grade
Kathy	71.5
Susan	93.5

This SELECT has both a WHERE and a HAVING clause. The WHERE ensures that you only select rows with a GradeType of "Quiz." The HAVING guarantees that you only select students with an average score of at least 70.

What if you wanted to add a column with the GradeType value? If you attempt to add GradeType to the SELECT *columnlist,* the statement will error. This is because all columns must be either listed in the GROUP BY or involved in an aggregation. If you want to show the GradeType column, it must be added to the GROUP BY clause, as follows:

```
SELECT
Student AS 'Student',
GradeType AS 'Grade Type',
AVG (Grade) AS 'Average Grade'
FROM Grades
WHERE GradeType = 'Quiz'
```

```
GROUP BY Student, GradeType
HAVING AVG (Grade) >= 70
ORDER BY Student
```

The resulting data is:

Student	Grade Type	Average Grade
Kathy	Quiz	71.5
Susan	Quiz	93.5

Now that we've added the `HAVING` clause to the mix, let's recap the general format of the `SELECT` statement:

```
SELECT columnlist
FROM tablelist
WHERE condition
GROUP BY columnlist
HAVING condition
ORDER BY columnlist
```

It should be emphasized that, when employing any of the above keywords in a `SELECT`, they need to be entered in the order shown. For example, the `HAVING` keyword needs to always be after a `GROUP BY` but before an `ORDER BY`.

Looking Ahead

In this chapter, we covered several forms of aggregation, starting with the simplest—that of eliminating duplicates. We then introduced a number of aggregate functions, which are a different class of functions from the scalar functions seen in Chapter 4. The real power of aggregate functions becomes apparent when they are used in conjunction with the `GROUP BY` keyword, which allows for true aggregation of data into groups. Finally, we covered the `HAVING` keyword, which allows you to apply group-level selection criteria to values in aggregate functions.

In our next chapter, "Combining Tables with an Inner Join," we're going to begin our exploration of a key topic in SQL, the ability to access data from multiple tables. Up until now, all `SELECT` queries have been against a single table. In the real world, this is an unrealistic scenario. The true value of relational databases lies in their ability to utilize multiple tables with related data. Seldom would one require data from only a single table.

The topic of accessing data from multiple tables will be directly addressed in Chapters 11 and 12. Chapter 11 covers the inner join and Chapter 12 looks at the outer join. Subsequently, Chapters 13 through 15 will explore variations on the same theme. After you complete the next five chapters, you will have mastered the essential techniques of obtaining data from multiple tables.

Chapter 11

Combining Tables with an Inner Join

Keywords Introduced: **INNER JOIN, ON**

Back in Chapter 1, we talked about the great advance of relational databases over their predecessors. The significant achievement of relational databases was their ability to allow data to be organized into any number of tables that are related but at the same time independent of each other. Unlike earlier databases, the relationships between tables in relational databases are not explicitly defined by a series of pointers. Instead, relationships are inferred by columns that tables have in common. Sometimes, these relationships are formalized by the definition of primary and foreign keys, but this isn't always necessary.

The great virtue of relational databases lies in the fact that someone can analyze business entities and then design an appropriate database design, which allows for maximum flexibility.

Let's look at a common example. Most organizations have a business entity known as the "customer." As such, it is typical for a database to contain a Customers table that defines each customer. Such a table would normally contain a primary key to uniquely identify each customer and any number of columns with attributes describing the customer. Common attributes might include phone number, address, city, state, and so on.

The main idea is that all information about the customer is stored in a single table and only in that table. This simplifies the task of data updates. When a customer changes his phone number, there is only one table that needs to be updated. However, the downside to this setup is that whenever someone needs any information about a customer, that person needs to access the Customers table to retrieve the information.

This brings us to the concept of a *join.* Let's say that someone is analyzing products that have been purchased. Along with information about the products, it is often necessary to provide information about the customers who purchased each product. For example, an analyst may desire to obtain customer ZIP codes for a geographic analysis. The ZIP code is only stored in the Customers table. Product information is stored in a Products table. To get information from both customers and products, the tables must be joined together in such a way that the information matches correctly.

In essence, the promise of relational databases is fulfilled by the ability to join tables together in any desired manner.

Joining Two Tables

To begin our exploration of the join process, let's revisit the Orders table that we first encountered in Chapter 3:

OrderID	FirstName	LastName	QuantityPurchased	PricePerItem
1	William	Smith	4	2.50
2	Natalie	Lopez	10	1.25
3	Brenda	Harper	5	4.00

The use of this table in earlier chapters was somewhat misleading. In reality, a competent database designer would never create a table such as this. The problem is that it contains information about two separate entities: customers and orders. In the real world, the information would be split into at least two separate tables. A Customers table might look like this:

CustomerID	FirstName	LastName
1	William	Smith
2	Natalie	Lopez
3	Brenda	Harper
4	Adam	Petrie

The Orders table would be similar to this:

OrderID	CustomerID	Quantity	PricePerItem
1	1	4	2.50
2	2	10	1.25
3	2	12	1.50
4	3	5	4.00

We'll be using these two tables for the examples in this chapter. Notice a number of additions. The Customers table now contains information only about customers. The Orders table now has information only about items purchased. We added a CustomerID column to the Orders table to tell which customer placed the order. As you might remember from Chapter 1, this is referred to as a *foreign key*. We also added a row to the Orders table to indicate one customer (Natalie Lopez) who placed more than one order. Additionally, we also added a new row to the Customers table to represent a potential customer (Adam Petrie) who has not yet placed an order.

Of course, there's much information that is still missing. For example, an Orders table would typically include additional columns, such as one that stores the order date. Also, an Orders table would typically have a foreign key column with a product ID, so the order could be linked to information about the product that was sold. Plus, the Orders table itself might, in fact, be split into more than one table so that information about the entire order (such as order date) could be stored separately from information about each item that was ordered (assuming that a customer could order more than one item in an order).

In other words, this still is not a completely realistic example. But now that we've split our information into two separate tables, we can address how to create a `SELECT` statement that can pull data from both tables simultaneously.

Before we get to the `SELECT` statement itself, we need to address one additional concern, which is how to represent visually the two tables and the implied relationship that exists between them. Previously, we displayed each table with the column names on the top row and corresponding data on subsequent rows. Now that we have more than one table to deal with, we're going to introduce another type of visual representation. Figure 11.1 shows a diagram with both tables, with the table name on the top row and the column names in each

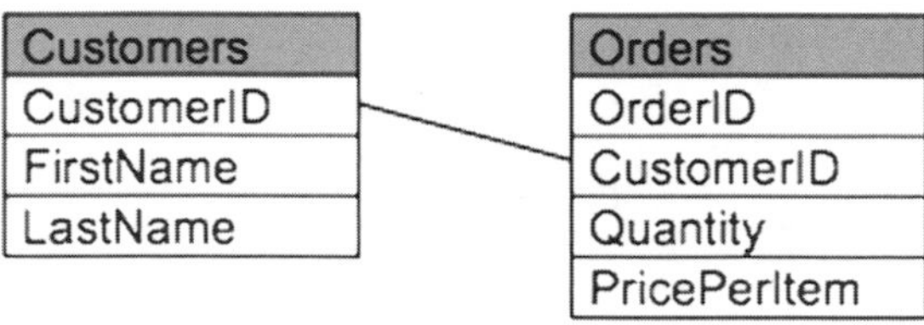

Figure 11.1
Entity-relationship diagram.

subsequent row. This diagram is a simplified version of what is commonly called an *entity-relationship* diagram. The term *entity* refers to the tables, and *relationship* refers to the lines drawn between the data elements in those tables.

The important point to notice is that we've drawn a line from CustomerID in the Customers table to CustomerID in the Orders table. This indicates that there is a relationship between these two tables. Both tables share values stored in the CustomerID column.

The Inner Join

We are now ready to present a `SELECT` statement with what is called an *inner join:*

```
SELECT *
FROM Customers
INNER JOIN Orders
ON Customers.CustomerID = Orders.CustomerID
```

Let's examine this statement line by line. The `SELECT` keyword on the first line merely states that we want all (*) columns from both tables. The second line, with the `FROM` clause, indicates that the first table we want to specify is the Customers table. The third line introduces a new `INNER JOIN` keyword. This keyword is used to specify an additional table that we want to join to. In this case, we want to add in the Orders table.

Finally, the fourth line introduces the `ON` keyword. The `ON` keyword works in conjunction with the `INNER JOIN`. The `ON` specifies exactly how the two tables are to be joined. In this case, we are connecting the CustomerID column of the Customers table (Customers.CustomerID) to the CustomerID column of the

Orders table (Orders.CustomerID). Since the CustomerID column has the same name in both the Customers and Orders table, we need to specify the table name as a prefix to the CustomerID column name in the `ON` clause. The prefix allows us to distinguish between these columns in two separate tables.

The above `SELECT` produces this data:

Customer ID	First Name	Last Name	Order ID	Customer ID	Quantity	PricePerItem
1	William	Smith	1	1	4	2.50
2	Natalie	Lopez	2	2	10	1.25
2	Natalie	Lopez	3	2	12	1.50
3	Brenda	Harper	4	3	5	4.00

Let's analyze the results. Both the Customers table and the Orders table had four rows. Looking at the OrderID column, you can tell that we have data from all four rows from the Orders table. However, looking at the CustomerID column, you might notice that we only have three customers shown. Why is that? The answer is that the customer with a CustomerID of 4 doesn't exist in the Orders table. Since we're joining the two tables together on the CustomerID field, we have no rows in the Orders table that match the CustomerID of 4 in the Customers table.

This brings us to this important observation: An inner join only brings back data for which there is a match between both tables being joined. In the next chapter, we'll talk about an alternative method of joining tables that will allow the customer information for CustomerID of 4 to be shown, even if there are no orders for this customer.

Here's a second important observation: Notice that the customer data for Natalie Lopez is repeated twice in the above results. She only existed once in the Customers table, so why is her customer data shown twice? The answer is that all possible matches are shown. Since Natalie has two rows in the Orders table, both of these rows match with her row in the Customers table, therefore bringing back her customer information twice.

Finally, you may be wondering why the join is referred to as an inner join. There are, in fact, two main variations of the join, the inner join and the outer join. Outer joins will be covered in the next chapter.

Table Order in Inner Joins

An inner join brings back data where there is a match between the two specified tables. In the previous SELECT, we specified the Customers table in the FROM clause and the Orders table in the INNER JOIN clause. But does it matter which table is specified first? As it turns out, the order in which the tables are listed can be reversed with no difference in the results. The following two SELECT statements are logically identical and bring back the same data:

```
SELECT *
FROM Customers
INNER JOIN Orders
ON Customers.CustomerID = Orders.CustomerID
```

```
SELECT *
FROM Orders
INNER JOIN Customers
ON Orders.CustomerID = Customers.CustomerID
```

The only difference is that the first statement would display columns from the Customers table first and the Orders table second. The second statement would show columns from the Orders table first and the Customers table second.

Remember that SQL is not a procedural language. It doesn't specify the exact order in which a task is to be completed. SQL only specifies the desired logic and leaves it to the internals of the database to decide exactly how to perform a task. As such, SQL doesn't determine exactly how the database physically retrieves data. The database software determines the optimal way of obtaining data for you.

Alternate Specification of Inner Joins

In the previous examples, we utilized the INNER JOIN and ON keywords to specify inner joins. It is also possible to specify inner joins with just the FROM and WHERE clauses.

You have already seen this statement that joins the Customers and Orders tables:

```
SELECT *
FROM Customers
INNER JOIN Orders
ON Customers.CustomerID = Orders.CustomerID
```

An alternate way of specifying the same inner join without the INNER JOIN and ON keywords is:

```
SELECT *
FROM Customers, Orders
WHERE Customers.CustomerID = Orders.CustomerID
```

In this alternate specification, rather than using the INNER JOIN keyword to specify additional tables to join, we merely list all tables to be joined in the FROM clause. Instead of using the ON clause to specify how the tables are related, we use the WHERE clause to specify the relationship between the tables.

Even though this alternate format works perfectly well and produces the same results, I don't recommend that it be used. The advantage of the INNER JOIN and ON keywords is that they explicitly present the logic of the join. That is their only purpose. Although it is possible to specify the relationship in a WHERE clause, the meaning of the SQL statement is less obvious when the WHERE clause is used for selection criteria and also to indicate relationships between multiple tables.

Table Aliases Revisited

Let's now look at the columns that were returned from the prior SELECT statement. Since we specified all (*) columns, you can see all columns from both tables. You can see the CustomerID column twice because that column exists in both tables. In practice, you would not want this data repeated. Here's an alternate version of the SELECT, which now specifies only the columns you want to see. In addition, let's now specify explicitly both table and column aliases. The table aliases (C for Customers and O for Orders) are specified right after the FROM and INNER JOIN keywords by inserting the AS keyword. The syntax now looks like:

```
SELECT
C.CustomerID AS 'Cust ID',
C.FirstName AS 'First Name',
C.LastName AS 'Last Name',
O.OrderID AS 'Order ID',
O.Quantity AS 'Qty',
O.PricePerItem AS 'Price'
FROM Customers AS C
INNER JOIN Orders AS O
ON C.CustomerID = O.CustomerID
```

The results are:

Cust ID	First Name	Last Name	Order ID	Qty	Price
1	William	Smith	1	4	2.50
2	Natalie	Lopez	2	10	1.25
2	Natalie	Lopez	3	12	1.50
3	Brenda	Harper	4	5	4.00

Notice that we're using the AS keyword to specify both column and table aliases. It should also be mentioned that the AS keyword is completely optional. All of the AS keywords can be removed from the SELECT, and the statement would still be valid and return the same results. However, I recommend the use of the AS keyword for the sake of clarity.

DATABASE DIFFERENCES: Oracle

As mentioned in Chapter 3, table aliases are specified in Oracle without the AS keyword. The syntax for the statement in Oracle is:

```
SELECT
C.CustomerID AS 'Cust ID',
C.FirstName AS 'First Name',
C.LastName AS 'Last Name',
O.OrderID AS 'Order ID',
O.Quantity AS 'Qty',
O.PricePerItem AS 'Price'
FROM Customers C
INNER JOIN Orders O
ON C.CustomerID = O.CustomerID;
```

Looking Ahead

The ability to join tables together in query is an essential feature of SQL. Relational databases would be of little use without joins. This chapter focused on the formulation of the inner join. The inner join brings back data for which there is a match between both tables being joined. We also talked about an alternate way of specifying the inner join and the usefulness of specifying table aliases.

In our next chapter, "Combining Tables with an Outer Join," we will turn to another important type of join, the outer join. As mentioned, inner joins only allow us to view data when there is a match between the tables being joined. So, if you have a customer with no orders, you won't see any customer information when doing an inner join between a Customers and an Orders table. The outer join will allow you to view customer information even if there are no orders for a customer. In other words, the outer join lets us see data that we would not otherwise be able to obtain with an inner join.

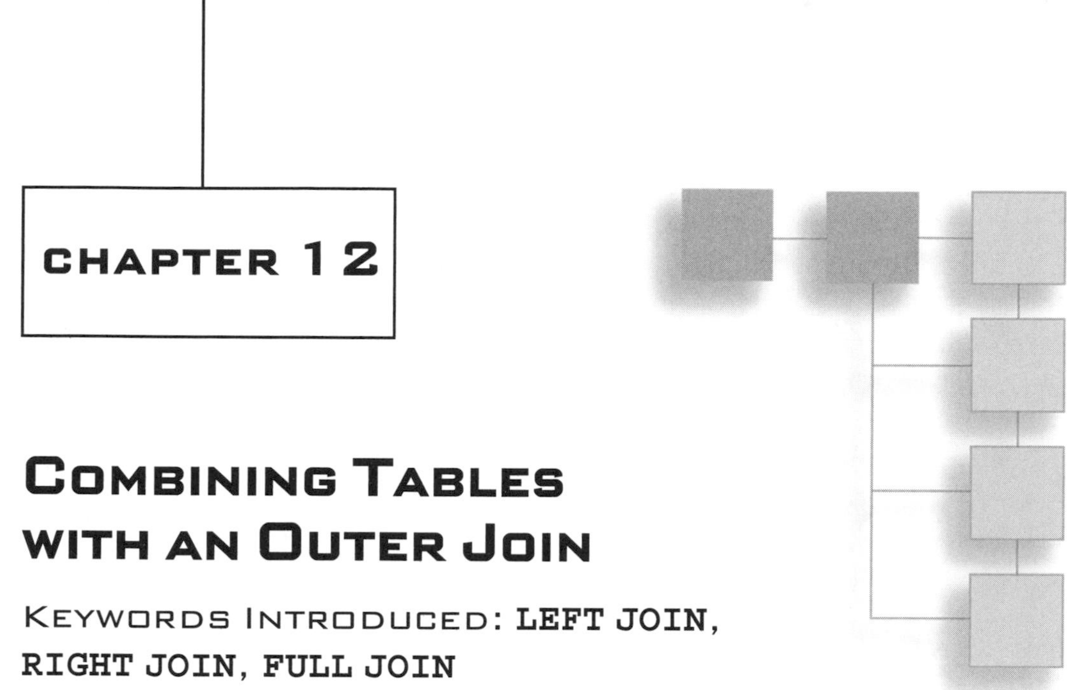

CHAPTER 12

Combining Tables with an Outer Join

KEYWORDS INTRODUCED: **LEFT JOIN, RIGHT JOIN, FULL JOIN**

We now advance from inner to outer joins. The main restriction of inner joins is that they require a match in all tables being joined to show any results. If you're joining a Customers table to an Orders table, no data for the customer is shown if that customer hasn't yet placed an order. This may seem like a relatively unimportant problem, but it often becomes more significant with different types of data.

Let's say, for example, that we have an Orders table and a Refunds table. The Refunds table is related to the Orders table by an OrderID. In other words, all refunds are tied to a specific order. The refund can't exist unless the order exists. The problem arises when you want to see both orders and refunds in a single query. If you join these two tables with an inner join, you won't see any orders if refunds were never issued against that order. Presumably, this will be the majority of your orders. In contrast, the outer join allows you to view orders even if they don't have a matching refund, and it is therefore an essential technique to understand and use.

The Outer Join

All the joins seen in the last chapter were inner joins. Since inner joins are the most common join type, SQL specifies these as a default, so you can specify an inner join using only the keyword `JOIN`. It isn't necessary to state `INNER JOIN`.

In contrast to inner joins, there are three types of outer joins: LEFT OUTER JOIN, RIGHT OUTER JOIN, and FULL OUTER JOIN. These can be referred to as simply: LEFT JOIN, RIGHT JOIN, and FULL JOIN. In this case, the word OUTER isn't necessary. To summarize, my recommendation is to refer to the four join types as:

- INNER JOIN
- LEFT JOIN
- RIGHT JOIN
- FULL JOIN

This keeps the syntax consistent and easy to remember.

In our discussion of outer joins, we're going to utilize three tables in our examples. First, there will be a Customers table with information about each customer. Second, there will be an Orders table with data on each order placed. Finally, we will add a Refunds table with information about any refunds that have been issued to customers.

Figure 12.1 shows how these three tables are connected.

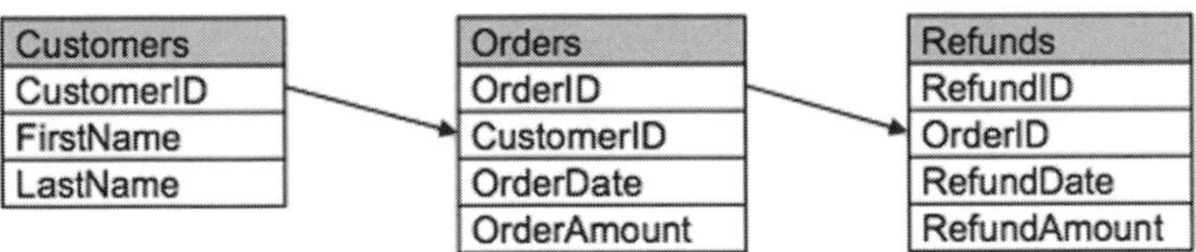

Figure 12.1
Entity-relationship diagram.

In contrast to the figure seen in the last chapter, the lines connecting the tables are now shown as arrows. You can see an arrow drawn from the CustomerID field of the Customers table to the CustomerID field of the Orders table. This arrow indicates that the link between the Customers and Orders tables is possibly one-sided in the sense that there may not be any orders for any given customer. Additionally, there may be multiple orders for a single customer. Similarly, the arrow drawn between the Orders and Refunds tables indicates that there may not be any refunds for any given order, and that there may be multiple refunds for an order.

The line between the Customers and Orders tables is on the CustomerID columns because the CustomerID is the common link between these two tables. Similarly, the line between the Orders and Refunds tables is on the OrderID columns because the OrderID is the common link between these two tables.

In other words, the Orders table is related to the Customers table by customer. There must be a customer for an order to exist. The Refunds table is related to the Orders table by the order. There must be an order before a refund is issued. Note that the Refunds table is not directly related to the Customers table. However, by joining all three tables together, we will be able to determine which customer a given refund was for.

Let's now examine the contents of each table. The Customers table has these values:

CustomerID	FirstName	LastName
1	William	Smith
2	Natalie	Lopez
3	Brenda	Harper
4	Adam	Petrie

The Orders table has this data:

OrderID	CustomerID	OrderDate	OrderAmount
1	1	2009-09-01	10.00
2	2	2009-09-02	12.50
3	2	2009-10-03	18.00
4	3	2009-09-15	20.00

The Refunds table contains this data:

RefundID	OrderID	RefundDate	RefundAmount
1	1	2009-09-02	5.00
2	3	2009-10-12	18.00

Notice that three out of the four customers have placed orders. Likewise, only two refunds have been issued for the four orders placed.

Left Joins

Let's now create a SELECT statement that joins all three tables together, using a LEFT JOIN:

```
SELECT
Customers.FirstName AS 'First Name',
Customers.LastName AS 'Last Name',
Orders.OrderDate AS 'Order Date',
Orders.OrderAmount AS 'Order Amt',
Refunds.RefundDate AS 'Refund Date',
Refunds.RefundAmount AS 'Refund Amt'
FROM Customers
LEFT JOIN Orders
ON Customers.CustomerID = Orders.CustomerID
LEFT JOIN Refunds
ON Orders.OrderID = Refunds.OrderID
ORDER BY Customers.CustomerID, Orders.OrderID, RefundID
```

The resulting data looks like:

First Name	Last Name	Order Date	Order Amt	Refund Date	Refund Amt
William	Smith	2009-09-01	10.00	2009-09-02	5.00
Natalie	Lopez	2009-09-02	12.50	NULL	NULL
Natalie	Lopez	2009-10-03	18.00	2009-10-12	18.00
Brenda	Harper	2009-09-15	20.00	NULL	NULL
Adam	Petrie	NULL	NULL	NULL	NULL

DATABASE DIFFERENCES: Oracle

Unlike SQL Server and MySQL, Oracle typically displays dates in a DD-MMM-YY format. For example, the date 2009-09-02 in the previous table will display as 02-SEP-09 in Oracle. However, no matter which database you're using, the exact format in which dates are displayed will vary, depending on how your database was set up.

Before analyzing the previous `SELECT` statement, notice that there are two interesting aspects of the data you can see. First, Adam Petrie has no data shown other than his name. The reason for the lack of data is that there are no rows in the Orders table associated with that customer. The power of the outer join comes from the fact that you can see some data for Adam Petrie, even if he has no orders. If we had specified an `INNER JOIN` rather than a `LEFT JOIN`, you would see no rows at all for Adam.

Similarly, you can see no refund data for either the 9/2/2009 order from Natalie Lopez or the order from Brenda Harper—because there are no rows in the Refunds table associated with those orders. If we had specified an `INNER JOIN` rather than a `LEFT JOIN`, you would see no rows for those two orders.

Let's now look at the `SELECT` statement itself. The first few lines that specify the columns are nothing that you haven't seen before. Notice that rather than using table aliases, we're listing all the columns with their full names, with the table as a prefix.

The first table listed is the Customers table. This table is shown after the `FROM` keyword. The second table shown is the Orders table, which appears after the first `LEFT JOIN` keyword. The subsequent `ON` clause specifies how the Orders table is linked to the Customers table. The third table shown is the Refunds table, which appears after the second `LEFT JOIN` keyword. The subsequent `ON` clause specifies how the Refunds table is joined to the Orders table.

It is critical to realize that the order in which tables are listed in reference to the `LEFT JOIN` keyword is significant. When specifying a `LEFT JOIN`, the table to the left of `LEFT JOIN` is always the *primary* table. The table to the right of the `LEFT JOIN` is the *secondary* table. When joining between the primary and secondary tables, we want all rows in the primary table, even if there are no matches with any rows in the secondary table.

In the first specified `LEFT JOIN`, the Customers table is on the left and the Orders table is on the right of the `LEFT JOIN`, which signifies that Customers is primary and Orders is secondary. In other words, we want to see all selected data from the Customers table, even if there isn't a corresponding match in the secondary table for that row.

Similarly, in the second `LEFT JOIN`, the Orders table is to the left and the Refunds table is to the right. That means that we are specifying Orders as primary and Refunds as secondary in this join. We want all orders, even if there are no matching refunds for that order.

Finally, we included an `ORDER BY` clause. Notice that the fields specified in the `ORDER BY` are not selected in the original *columnlist*.

Testing for NULL Values

In the previous `SELECT`, we had one customer with no orders and two orders with no associated refunds. Unlike the `INNER JOIN`, the `LEFT JOIN` allows these rows with missing values to appear.

To test your understanding of the `LEFT JOIN`, let's now ask how we would list only those orders for which *no* refund was issued. The solution involves adding a `WHERE` clause that tests for NULL values, as follows:

```
SELECT
Customers.FirstName AS 'First Name',
Customers.LastName AS 'Last Name',
Orders.OrderDate AS 'Order Date',
Orders.OrderAmount AS 'Order Amt'
FROM Customers
LEFT JOIN Orders
ON Customers.CustomerID = Orders.CustomerID
LEFT JOIN Refunds
ON Orders.OrderID = Refunds.OrderID
WHERE Orders.OrderID IS NOT NULL
AND Refunds.RefundID IS NULL
ORDER BY Customers.CustomerID, Orders.OrderID
```

The resulting data is:

First Name	Last Name	Order Date	Order Amt
Natalie	Lopez	2009-09-02	12.50
Brenda	Harper	2009-09-15	20.00

The `WHERE` clause first tests Orders.OrderID to make sure that it isn't NULL. Doing so ensures that you don't see customers who never placed an order. The second portion of the `WHERE` clause tests Refunds.RefundID to make sure that it is NULL. This ensures that you only see orders that don't match a refund.

Right Joins

The previous SELECT statements utilized the LEFT JOIN keyword. The good news about right joins is that they are identical in concept to the left join. The only difference between left and right joins is the order in which the two tables in the join are listed.

In left joins, the primary table is listed to the left of the LEFT JOIN keyword. The secondary table, which may or may not contain matching rows, is listed to the right of the LEFT JOIN keyword.

In right joins, the primary table is listed to the right of the RIGHT JOIN keyword. The secondary table is listed to the left of the RIGHT JOIN keyword. That's the only difference.

The FROM clause of the previous SELECT statement was:

```
FROM Customers
LEFT JOIN Orders
ON Customers.CustomerID = Orders.CustomerID
LEFT JOIN Refunds
ON Orders.OrderID = Refunds.OrderID
```

If we desire to restate this using right joins, we could change it to:

```
FROM Refunds
RIGHT JOIN Orders
ON Orders.OrderID = Refunds.OrderID
RIGHT JOIN Customers
ON Customers.CustomerID = Orders.CustomerID
```

The point to note is that it's only the order in which tables are listed before and after the RIGHT JOIN that matters. The order in which columns are listed after the ON keyword has no significance.

Basically, this means that it's completely unnecessary to ever use the RIGHT JOIN keyword. Anything that can be specified with a RIGHT JOIN can be specified with a LEFT JOIN. Our suggestion is to stick with the LEFT JOIN, since we intuitively tend to think in terms of listing more important, or primary, tables first.

Table Order in Outer Joins

We previously noted that the order in which tables were specified in an inner join was not material. The same is *not* true of outer joins, since the order that tables are listed in a left or right join *is* significant. However, there is some flexibility in listing the tables in situations where there are three or more tables. The order of the left (or right) join keywords can be switched around if desired.

Let's again look at the original FROM clause from the previous SELECT:

```
FROM Customers
LEFT JOIN Orders
ON Customers.CustomerID = Orders.CustomerID
LEFT JOIN Refunds
ON Orders.OrderID = Refunds.OrderID
```

We've already seen that you can list the Refunds table first and the Customers table last, as long as you convert everything to right joins, as in:

```
FROM Refunds
RIGHT JOIN Orders
ON Orders.OrderID = Refunds.OrderID
RIGHT JOIN Customers
ON Customers.CustomerID = Orders.CustomerID
```

Is it possible to list the Customers table first and then the Refunds table, followed by the Orders table? Yes, as long as you're willing to mix left and right joins together and throw in some parentheses. The following is equivalent to the above:

```
FROM Customers
LEFT JOIN (Refunds
RIGHT JOIN Orders
ON Orders.OrderID = Refunds.OrderID)
ON Customers.CustomerID = Orders.CustomerID
```

What was originally a fairly simple statement has now turned into something unnecessarily complex. Our advice is to stick with the LEFT JOIN keyword and avoid parentheses when devising complex FROM clauses with multiple tables.

Full Joins

The remaining outer join type is the full join. You've seen that in left and right joins, one table is primary and the other one is secondary. Alternatively, you can say that one table is required and one is optional, which means that when matching two tables, rows in the secondary (or optional) table don't necessarily have to exist.

In the inner join, both tables are primary (or required). When matching two tables, there has to be a match between both tables for a row of data to be selected.

In the full join, both tables are secondary (or optional). In this situation, if we're matching rows in table A and table B, then we display 1) all rows from table A, even if there is no matching row in table B, and also 2) all rows from table B, even if there is no matching row in table A.

DATABASE DIFFERENCES: MySQL

Unlike Microsoft SQL Server and Oracle, MySQL doesn't provide for a full join.

Let's look at an example involving matching rows from these two tables. First, a Movies table:

MovieID	MovieTitle	Rating
1	Sleepless in Seattle	PG
2	Lost in America	R
3	Bambi	G
4	North by Northwest	Not Rated
5	Forrest Gump	PG-13
6	The Truman Show	PG

Second, a Ratings table:

RatingID	Rating	RatingDescription
1	G	General Audiences
2	PG	Parental Guidance Suggested
3	PG-13	Parents Strongly Cautioned
4	R	Restricted
5	NC-17	No One 17 and Under Admitted

The Movies table has a list of movies in the database and includes the MPAA rating for each movie. The Ratings table has a list of the ratings and their descriptions. Let's say you want to find all matches between these two tables. You're going to use a `FULL JOIN` to show all rows from the Movies table, as well as all rows from the Ratings table. The full join will show all rows, even if a match from the other table isn't found. The SELECT looks like:

```
SELECT
MovieTitle AS 'Movie',
RatingDescription AS 'Rating Description'
FROM Movies
FULL JOIN Ratings
ON Movies.Rating = Ratings.Rating
ORDER BY RatingDescription, MovieTitle
```

The result of this statement is:

Movie	Rating Description
North by Northwest	NULL
Bambi	General Audience
NULL	No One 17 and Under Admitted
Sleepless in Seattle	Parental Guidance Suggested
The Truman Show	Parental Guidance Suggested
Forrest Gump	Parents Strongly Cautioned
Lost in America	Restricted

Notice that there are two blank cells in the data, which is a direct result of having used a FULL JOIN. In the first instance, there is no rating shown for *North by Northwest* because there was no matching row in the Ratings table for that movie. In the second instance, there is no movie shown for the "No One 17 and Under Admitted" rating description because there were no matching rows in the Movies table for that rating.

The full join is seldom used in practice for the simple reason that this type of relationship between tables is relatively uncommon. In essence, the full join shows data where there are nonmatches in both directions between two tables. We are normally only interested in data where there is a complete match between two tables (the inner join) or perhaps a one-sided match (the left or right join).

Looking Ahead

This chapter extended our discussion of joins to left, right, and full joins. The left join enables you to join a primary and a secondary table together. The left join shows all rows in the primary table, even if there is no match in the secondary table. The right join is simply the reverse of the left join, switching the order of the primary and secondary tables. Finally, the full join enables both tables to be secondary tables. It displays all rows that are in either table, even if there isn't a match in the other table.

In our next chapter, "Self Joins and Views," we're going to take a slight detour to two related topics. First, we're going to talk about self joins, which is a special technique that allows us to join a table to itself. In a way, this creates a virtual view of the table, in the sense that we can now view this table from two different perspectives. The second main topic of the next chapter will extend the concept of self joins to a more general way of creating virtual views of multiple tables.

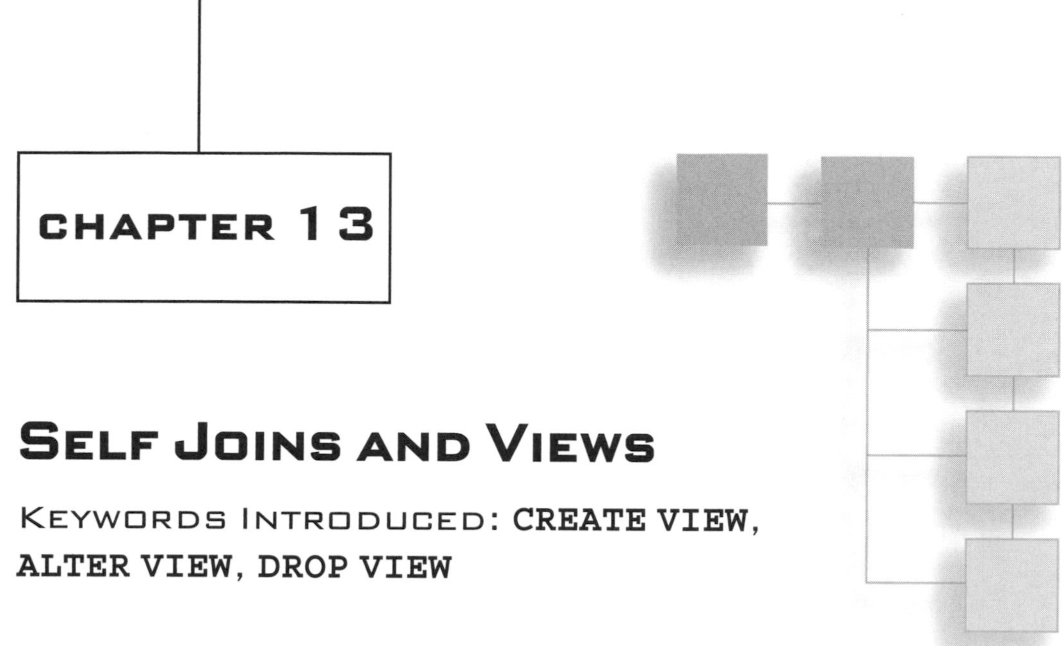

CHAPTER 13

Self Joins and Views

Keywords Introduced: **CREATE VIEW, ALTER VIEW, DROP VIEW**

The inner and outer joins of the past two chapters have dealt with various ways of combining data from multiple tables. We're now going to examine alternate ways of using and defining tables. Previously, we've always assumed that the data we're looking at physically exists in tables in a database. We'll now turn to two techniques that will let us view data in a virtual way.

The first technique, the self join, allows you to refer to the same table twice, as if it were two separate tables. In essence, the self join creates a virtual view of a table, allowing it to be used more than once.

Second, you'll learn about database views, which are a useful concept that enables you to create new virtual tables at will.

Self Joins

The self join lets you join a table to itself. The most common use of the self join is to deal with tables that are self-referencing in nature. These are tables that have a column that refers to another column in the same table. A common example of this type of relationship is a table that contains information about employees.

In this example, each row in a Personnel table has a column that points to another row in the same table, representing the employee's manager. In some ways, this is similar to the concept of foreign keys. The main difference is that, whereas foreign keys point to columns in other tables, we now have columns that point to rows in the same table.

Let's look at the data in this Personnel table:

EmployeeID	EmployeeName	ManagerID
1	Susan Ford	NULL
2	Harold Jenkins	1
3	Jacqueline Baker	1
4	Richard Fielding	1
5	Carol Bland	2
6	Janet Midling	2
7	Andrew Brown	3
8	Anne Nichol	4
9	Bradley Cash	4
10	David Sweet	5

The ManagerID column tells which manager the employee reports to. The ID number in this column corresponds to the numbers in the EmployeeID column. For example, Harold Jenkins has a ManagerID of 1. This indicates that Harold's manager is Susan Ford, who has an EmployeeID of 1.

Similarly, it can be seen that the three people who report to Susan Ford are Harold Jenkins, Jacqueline Baker, and Richard Fielding. Notice that Susan Ford has no value in the ManagerID column. This indicates that she is the head of the company. She has no manager.

Now, let's say that we want to list all employees and show the name of the manager who each employee reports to. To accomplish this, we're going to create a self join of the Employees table to itself. A table alias must always be used with self joins so you have a way of distinguishing each instance of the table. The first instance of the table will be given a table alias of Employees, and the second instance will be given a table alias of Managers. Here's the statement:

```
SELECT
Employees.EmployeeName AS 'Employee Name',
Managers.EmployeeName AS 'Manager Name'
FROM Personnel AS Employees
INNER JOIN Personnel AS Managers
ON Employees.ManagerID = Managers.EmployeeID
ORDER BY Employees.EmployeeID
```

The resulting data is:

Employee Name	Manager Name
Harold Jenkins	Susan Ford
Jacqueline Baker	Susan Ford
Richard Fielding	Susan Ford
Carol Bland	Harold Jenkins
Janet Midling	Harold Jenkins
Andrew Brown	Jacqueline Baker
Anne Nichol	Richard Fielding
Bradley Cash	Richard Fielding
David Sweet	Carol Bland

The trickiest part of this `SELECT` is the `ON` clause in the join. To get the self join to work correctly, we need to use the `ON` to establish a relationship between the ManagerID column of the Employees view of the Personnel table and the EmployeeID column of the Managers view of the table. In other words, the indicated manager is also an employee.

Notice that Susan Ford isn't shown in the previous data because we utilized an inner join in the statement. Since Susan Ford has no manager, there is no match to the Managers view of the table. If we want Susan to be included, we merely need to change the line:

```
INNER JOIN Personnel AS Managers
```

to:

```
LEFT JOIN Personnel AS Managers
```

The data retrieved is then:

Employee Name	Manager Name
Susan Ford	NULL
Harold Jenkins	Susan Ford
Jacqueline Baker	Susan Ford
Richard Fielding	Susan Ford
Carol Bland	Harold Jenkins
Janet Midling	Harold Jenkins

(continued)

Employee Name	Manager Name
Andrew Brown	Jacqueline Baker
Anne Nichol	Richard Fielding
Bradley Cash	Richard Fielding
David Sweet	Carol Bland

Creating Views

The self join allows you to create multiple views of the same table. We're now going to extend this concept to the ability to create new views of any table or any combination of tables.

Views are merely `SELECT` statements that have been saved in a database. Once saved, the view can be referred to the same as any table in the database. Database tables contain physical data. Views do not contain data, but allow you to proceed as if the view were a real table with data.

Why are views necessary? We'll get into the benefits of views in detail later in the chapter, but in short, the answer is that views provide added flexibility as to how you can access data. Whether your database has been around for one day or for years, your data is stored in tables in that database in a very specific manner. As time moves on, requirements for accessing that data change, but it isn't always easy to reorganize the data in your database to meet new requirements. The great advantage of views is that they allow you to create new virtual views of the data that is already in your database. Views enable you to create the equivalent of new tables without actually having to physically rearrange data. As such, views add a dynamic element to your ability to keep your database design fresh and up to date.

How is a view stored in a database? All relational databases consist of a number of different object types. The most important type is the table. However, most database management software allows users to save any number of other object types. The most common of these are views and stored procedures. There are often many other object types in a database. For example, Microsoft SQL Server allows users to create many other object types, such as functions and triggers.

SQL provides the `CREATE VIEW` keyword to enable users to create new views. The syntax is as follows:

```
CREATE VIEW ViewName AS
SelectStatement
```

After the view is created, the *ViewName* is used to reference the data that would be returned from the *SelectStatement* in the view.

Here's an example. In the last chapter, we looked at this `SELECT` statement:

```
SELECT
Customers.FirstName AS 'First Name',
Customers.LastName AS 'Last Name',
Orders.OrderDate AS 'Order Date',
Orders.OrderAmount AS 'Order Amt',
Refunds.RefundDate AS 'Refund Date',
Refunds.RefundAmount AS 'Refund Amt'
FROM Customers
LEFT JOIN Orders
ON Customers.CustomerID = Orders.CustomerID
LEFT JOIN Refunds
ON Orders.OrderID = Refunds.OrderID
ORDER BY Customers.CustomerID, Orders.OrderID, RefundID
```

This statement returned this data:

First Name	Last Name	Order Date	Order Amt	Refund Date	Refund Amt
William	Smith	2009-09-01	10.00	2009-09-02	5.00
Natalie	Lopez	2009-09-02	12.50	NULL	NULL
Natalie	Lopez	2009-10-03	18.00	2009-10-12	18.00
Brenda	Harper	2009-09-15	20.00	NULL	NULL
Adam	Petrie	NULL	NULL	NULL	NULL

How would we set up this `SELECT` statement as a view? We simply place the entire `SELECT` statement in a `CREATE VIEW` statement as follows:

```
CREATE VIEW CustomersOrdersRefunds AS
SELECT
Customers.FirstName AS 'First Name',
Customers.LastName AS 'Last Name',
Orders.OrderDate AS 'Order Date',
Orders.OrderAmount AS 'Order Amt',
Refunds.RefundDate AS 'Refund Date',
Refunds.RefundAmount AS 'Refund Amt'
```

```
FROM Customers
LEFT JOIN Orders
ON Customers.CustomerID = Orders.CustomerID
LEFT JOIN Refunds
ON Orders.OrderID = Refunds.OrderID
```

The only item missing in the above `CREATE VIEW` is the `ORDER BY` clause of the original `SELECT` statement. Since views aren't stored as physical data, there is no point in including an `ORDER BY` clause in a view.

Referencing Views

When we execute the above `CREATE VIEW` statement, it creates a view called CustomersOrdersRefunds. Creating the view does not return any data. It merely defines the view for later use.

To use the view to bring back the same data as before, we execute this `SELECT` statement:

```
SELECT *
FROM CustomersOrdersRefunds
```

This retrieves:

First Name	Last Name	Order Date	Order Amt	Refund Date	Refund Amt
William	Smith	2009-09-01	10.00	2009-09-02	5.00
Natalie	Lopez	2009-09-02	12.50	NULL	NULL
Natalie	Lopez	2009-10-03	18.00	2009-10-12	18.00
Brenda	Harper	2009-09-15	20.00	NULL	NULL
Adam	Petrie	NULL	NULL	NULL	NULL

What if you only wanted to see a few columns from the view for one specific customer? You could issue a `SELECT` statement such as:

```
SELECT
[First Name],
[Last Name],
[Order Date]
FROM CustomersOrdersRefunds
WHERE [Last Name] = 'Lopez'
```

The output is:

First Name	Last Name	Order Date
Natalie	Lopez	2009-09-02
Natalie	Lopez	2009-10-03

It is important to note that when you reference columns in this view, you need to specify the column alias names that were specified when the view was created. You can no longer reference original column names. For example, the view assigns a column alias named 'First Name' for the Customers.FirstName column. In Microsoft SQL Server, these column aliases are enclosed in square brackets due to the embedded spaces in the names.

DATABASE DIFFERENCES: MySQL and Oracle

As discussed in Chapter 2, MySQL and Oracle use different characters around columns containing spaces. MySQL uses the accent grave (`); Oracle uses double quotes (").

Benefits of Views

The previous example illustrates one of the important benefits of using views. Once a view is created, that view can be referenced just like it was a table. Even if the view were created from multiple tables joined together, it now appears, logically, to be just one table.

Let's summarize the benefits of using views:

- **Views can reduce complexity.** First, views can simplify `SELECT` statements that are particularly complex. For example, if you have a `SELECT` statement that joins six tables together, it may be useful to create views with two or three tables each. You can reference those views in a `SELECT` statement that is less complex than the original.
- **Views can increase reusability.** If you have a situation where three tables are always joined together, you can create a view with those three tables. Then, instead of always having to join those three tables every time you need data from those tables, you can simply reference a predefined view.

- **Views can properly format data.** If you have a column that is not formatted correctly in your database, you can use the `CAST` or other functions to format that column exactly as you want. For example, you may have a date column that is stored as an integer datatype in your database in a YYYYMMDD format. Users may prefer to view this data as a date/time column so it can be presented and used as a true date. To accomplish this, a view can be created on the table, which transforms that column to the proper format. Then all subsequent references to that table can reference the new view rather than the table.
- **Views can create calculated columns.** Let's say that you have two columns in a table: Quantity and PricePerItem. Your users are usually interested in TotalPrice data, which is found by multiplying the two columns together. You can create a view of the original table easily with a new calculated column that contains this calculation. Users can then reference the new view and always have the calculation available.
- **Views can be used to rename column names.** If your database contains cryptic column names, you can create views with column aliases to translate those names into something more meaningful.
- **Views can create a subset of data.** Let's say you have a table with all your customers. Most of your users only need to see customers who have placed an order during the past year. You can easily create a view that has this useful subset of data.
- **Views can be used to enforce security restrictions.** You may have a situation where you want certain users to be able to access only certain columns in a given table. To accomplish this, you can create a view of the table for those users. You can then use the security features of your database to grant access to the new view for those users, while restricting them from accessing the underlying table.

Modifying and Deleting Views

After a view is created, it can be modified easily by using the `ALTER VIEW` statement. Here's the syntax:

```
ALTER VIEW ViewName AS
SelectStatement
```

When altering a view, you need to completely specify the entire SELECT statement contained in the view. The original SELECT in the view gets replaced by the new SELECT that you specify.

Let's say that you originally created a view with this statement:

```
CREATE VIEW CustomersView AS
SELECT
FirstName AS 'First Name',
LastName AS 'Last Name'
FROM Customers
```

If you now want to modify the view to add a new column for middle name, you can issue a statement such as:

```
ALTER VIEW CustomersView AS
SELECT
FirstName AS 'First Name',
MiddleName AS 'Middle Name',
LastName AS 'Last Name'
FROM Customers
```

Once again, creating or altering a view does not return any data. It merely creates or modifies the definition of the view.

DATABASE DIFFERENCES: Oracle

Unlike Microsoft SQL Server and MySQL, the ALTER VIEW command in Oracle is more restrictive. To accomplish the previous ALTER VIEW in Oracle, you would need to issue a DROP VIEW and then a CREATE VIEW with the new view definition.

The DROP VIEW statement is used to delete a view you previously created. The syntax is:

```
DROP VIEW ViewName
```

If you want to delete the CustomersView view you created earlier, you can issue this statement:

```
DROP VIEW CustomersView
```

Looking Ahead

Self joins and views are two different ways to view data in a virtual manner. The self join allows you to join a table to itself. Views are much more flexible.

Essentially, any `SELECT` statement can be saved as a view, which can then be referenced like any normal table. Unlike tables, views do not contain any data. They merely define a new virtual view of data in existing tables. Views serve a wide variety of functions, from reducing complexity to reformatting data. Once created, views can be modified or deleted with the `ALTER VIEW` and `DELETE VIEW` statements.

In our next chapter, "Subqueries," we are going to return to a topic more directly related to our prior discussion of how to join tables together. Subqueries provide a method of relating tables to each other without making explicit use of an inner or outer join. Due to the wide variety of types of subqueries and ways in which they can be used, this is probably the most difficult but potentially rewarding subject in this book. There's actually quite a bit of flexibility as to how and when subqueries can be used. As such, this is something that lends itself to a certain amount of creativity in your query designs.

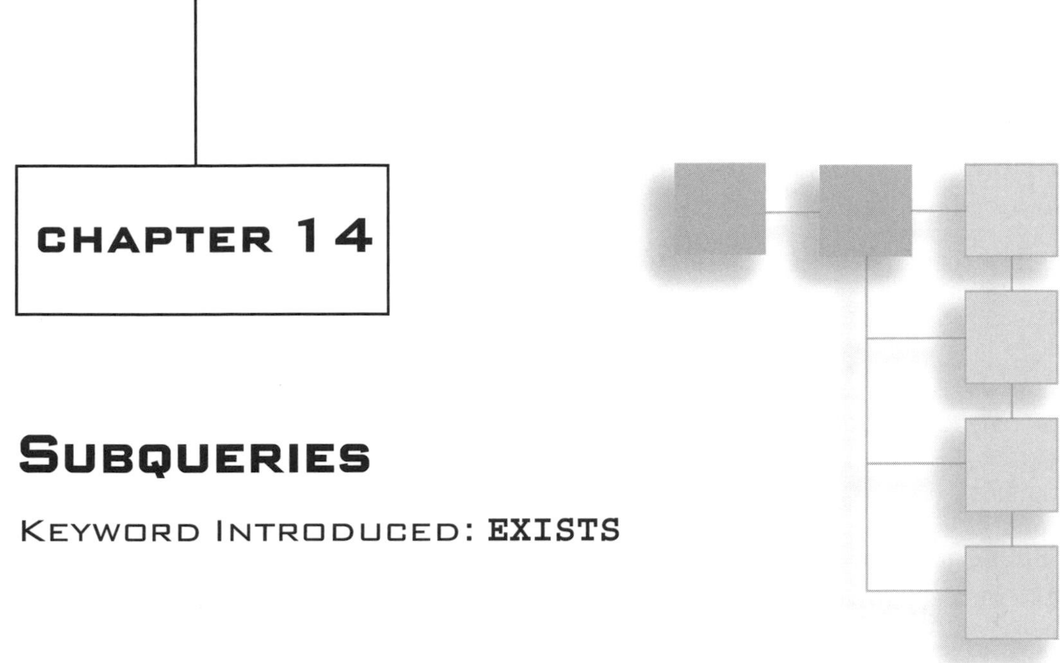

Chapter 14

Subqueries

Keyword Introduced: **EXISTS**

In Chapter 4, we talked about composite functions. These were functions that contained other functions. In a similar manner, it is possible for SQL queries to contain other queries. The queries that are contained within other queries are called *subqueries*.

The topic of subqueries is somewhat complex, primarily because there are many different ways in which they can be used. Subqueries can be found in many different parts of the `SELECT` statement, each with different nuances and requirements. As a query contained within another query, subqueries can be related to and dependent on the main query, or they can be completely independent of the main query. Again, this distinction results in different usage requirements.

No matter how subqueries are used, they add a great deal of flexibility to the ways in which you can write SQL queries. It many cases, subqueries provide functionality that could be accomplished by other means. In such instances, personal preferences will come into play as you decide whether or not you want to utilize the subquery solution. However, as you will see, there are certain situations where subqueries are absolutely essential for the task at hand.

With that, let's begin our discussion with an outline of the basic types of subqueries.

Types of Subqueries

Subqueries can be utilized not only with `SELECT` statements, but also with the `INSERT`, `UPDATE`, and `DELETE` statements, which will be covered in

Chapter 17. In this chapter, however, we're going to restrict our discussion of subqueries to the `SELECT`.

Here's the general `SELECT` statement that we have seen:

```
SELECT columnlist
FROM tablelist
WHERE condition
GROUP BY columnlist
HAVING condition
ORDER BY columnlist
```

Subqueries can be inserted into virtually any of the clauses in the `SELECT` statement. However, the way in which the subquery is stated and used varies slightly, depending on whether it is used in a *columnlist*, a *tablelist*, or a *condition*.

But what exactly is a subquery? A subquery is merely a `SELECT` statement that is inserted inside another `SELECT` statement. Additionally, a `SELECT` statement can have more than one subquery.

To sum up, there are three main ways in which subqueries can be specified:

- When a subquery is part of a *tablelist*, it specifies a data source.
- When a subquery is part of a *condition*, it becomes part of the selection criteria.
- When a subquery is part of a *columnlist*, it creates a single calculated column.

The remainder of this chapter will explain each of these three scenarios in detail.

Using a Subquery as a Data Source

When a subquery is specified as part of the `FROM` clause, it instantly creates a new data source. This is similar to the concept of creating a view and then referencing that view in a `SELECT`. The only difference is that a view is permanently saved in a database. A subquery used as a data source isn't saved. It exists only temporarily, as part of the `SELECT` statement.

We will first consider an example that illustrates how subqueries can be used as data sources. Let's say we have this Customers table:

CustomerID	CustomerName
1	William Smith
2	Natalie Lopez
3	Brenda Harper
4	Adam Petrie

Also, this Orders table:

OrderID	CustomerID	OrderAmount	OrderType
1	1	22.25	Cash
2	2	11.75	Credit
3	2	5.00	Credit
4	2	8.00	Cash
5	3	9.33	Credit
6	3	10.11	Credit

We would like to see a list of customers, along with a total sum of the cash orders they have placed. The following SELECT accomplishes that task:

```
SELECT
CustomerName AS 'Customer Name',
ISNULL (CashOrders.SumOfOrders, 0) AS 'Total Cash Orders'
FROM Customers
LEFT JOIN

(SELECT
CustomerID,
SUM (OrderAmount) as 'SumOfOrders'
FROM Orders
WHERE OrderType = 'Cash'
GROUP BY CustomerID) AS CashOrders

ON Customers.CustomerID = CashOrders.CustomerID
ORDER BY Customers.CustomerID
```

Two blank lines were inserted to clearly separate the subquery from the rest of the statement. The subquery is the middle section of the statement.

The results were:

Customer Name	Total Cash Orders
William Smith	22.25
Natalie Lopez	8.00
Brenda Harper	0
Adam Petrie	0

Adam Petrie shows no cash orders, since he didn't place any orders. Even though Brenda Harper placed two orders, they were both credit orders, so she also shows no cash orders. Note that the `ISNULL` function converts the NULL values that would normally appear for Adam and Brenda to a 0.

Let's now analyze how the subquery works. The subquery in the previous statement is:

```
SELECT
CustomerID,
SUM (OrderAmount) as 'Total Cash Orders'
FROM Orders
WHERE OrderType = 'Cash'
GROUP BY CustomerID
```

In general form, the main `SELECT` statement in the above is:

```
SELECT
CustomerName AS 'Customer Name',
ISNULL (OrderCounts.SumOfOrders, 0) AS 'Total Cash Orders'
FROM
Customers
INNER JOIN
(subquery) AS CashOrders
ON Customers.CustomerID = CashOrders.CustomerID
ORDER BY Customers.CustomerID
```

If the subquery were executed by itself, the results would be:

CustomerID	SumOfOrders
1	2.25
2	8

We only see data for customers 1 and 2. The `WHERE` clause in the subquery enforces the restriction that we only look at cash orders.

In this example, the entire subquery is referenced as if it were a separate table or view. Notice that the subquery is given a table alias of CashOrders, which allows the columns in the subquery to be referenced in the main `SELECT`. As such, the following line in the main `SELECT` references data in the subquery:

```
ISNULL (CashOrders.SumOfOrders, 0) AS 'Total Cash Orders'
```

CashOrders.SumOfOrders is a column that is taken from the subquery.

Is it truly necessary to use a subquery to obtain the desired data? In this case, the answer is yes. We might have attempted to simply join the Customers and Orders tables via a left join, as in the following:

```
SELECT
CustomerName AS 'Customer Name',
Sum (OrderAmount) AS 'Total Cash Orders'
FROM Customers
LEFT JOIN Orders
ON Customers.CustomerID = Orders.CustomerID
WHERE OrderType = 'Cash'
GROUP BY Customers.CustomerID, CustomerName
ORDER BY Customers.CustomerID
```

However, this statement yields the following data:

Customer Name	Total Cash Orders
William Smith	22.25
Natalie Lopez	8.00

We no longer see any rows for Brenda Harper or Adam Petrie, because the `WHERE` clause exclusion for cash orders is now in the main query rather than in a subquery. As a result, we no longer see any rows for customers who didn't place cash orders.

Using a Subquery in Selection Criteria

In Chapter 8, we introduced the first format of the `IN` operator. The example we used was:

```
WHERE State IN ('IL', 'NY')
```

In this format, the IN operator merely lists a number of values in parentheses. There is also a second format for the IN, one in which an entire SELECT statement is inserted inside the parentheses. For example, a list of states might be specified as:

```
WHERE State IN
(SELECT
States
FROM StateTable
WHERE Region = 'Midwest')
```

Rather than list individual states, the second format allows us to generate a list of states through more complex logic.

Let's illustrate with an example that uses our Customers and Orders tables. Let's say we want to retrieve a list of customers who have ever paid cash for any order they've placed. A SELECT that accomplishes this is:

```
SELECT CustomerName AS 'Customer Name'
FROM Customers
WHERE CustomerID IN
(SELECT CustomerID
FROM Orders
WHERE OrderType = 'Cash')
```

The resulting data is:

Customer Name
William Smith
Natalie Lopez

Brenda Harper is not included in the list because she has never placed an order using cash. Notice that a subquery SELECT is placed entirely within the parentheses for the IN keyword. Also note that the CustomerID column is used to connect the two queries. Even though we are displaying CustomerName, we use CustomerID to define the relationship between the Customers and Orders tables.

Once again, we can ask whether this subquery can also be expressed as a normal query, and the answer is yes. Here is an equivalent query that returns the same data:

```
SELECT CustomerName AS 'Customer Name'
FROM Customers
INNER JOIN Orders
ON Customers.CustomerID = Orders.CustomerID
WHERE OrderType = 'Cash'
GROUP BY Customers.CustomerID, Customers.CustomerName
```

Without using a subquery, we can directly join the Customers and Orders table. However, a `GROUP BY` clause is now needed to ensure that we only bring back one row per customer.

Correlated Subqueries

The subqueries we've seen so far have been uncorrelated subqueries. Generally speaking, all subqueries can be classified as either *uncorrelated* or *correlated*. These terms describe whether the subquery is related to the query in which it is contained. Uncorrelated subqueries are unrelated. When a subquery is unrelated, that means that it is completely independent of the outer query. Uncorrelated queries are evaluated and executed only once as part of the entire `SELECT` statement.

In contrast, correlated subqueries are specifically related to the outer query. Because of this explicit relationship, correlated subqueries need to be evaluated for each row returned and can produce different results each time the subquery is executed.

The best way to explain is with an example. Returning to the Customers and Orders tables, let's say we want to produce a list of customers who have a total order amount that is less than 20 dollars. Here's a statement that accomplishes that request:

```
SELECT
CustomerName as 'Customer Name'
FROM Customers
WHERE
(SELECT
SUM (OrderAmount)
FROM Orders
WHERE Customers.CustomerID = Orders.CustomerID)
< 20
```

The result is:

Customer Name
Brenda Harper

What makes this subquery correlated, as opposed to uncorrelated? The answer can be seen by looking at the subquery itself:

```
SELECT
SUM (OrderAmount)
FROM Orders
WHERE Customers.CustomerID = Orders.CustomerID
```

This subquery is correlated because it cannot be executed on its own. If run by itself, this subquery would error because the Customers.CustomerID column doesn't exist within the context of the subquery.

To understand what's going on, it's helpful to look at the entire SELECT statement in a general way:

```
SELECT
CustomerName as 'Customer Name'
FROM Customers
WHERE
SubqueryResult < 20
```

As a correlated subquery, the subquery needs to be evaluated for each customer. Also note that this type of subquery only works if it returns a single value.

Again, one might ask if this subquery could be converted into a normal SELECT statement. In this case, it can. Here's an equivalent statement that produces the same results:

```
SELECT
CustomerName as 'Customer Name'
FROM Customers
LEFT JOIN Orders
ON Customers.CustomerID = Orders.CustomerID
GROUP BY Customers.CustomerID, CustomerName
HAVING SUM (OrderAmount) < 20
```

Notice that, without a subquery, the equivalent statement now requires GROUP BY and HAVING clauses. The GROUP BY clause creates groups of customers, and the HAVING clause enforces the requirement that each group must have ordered less than 20 dollars.

The EXISTS Operator

One additional technique associated with correlated subqueries is the use of a special operator called EXISTS. This operator allows you to determine if data in a correlated subquery exists. Let's say that you want to discover which customers have placed orders. One way of accomplishing that is with this statement:

```
SELECT
CustomerName AS 'Customer Name'
FROM Customers
WHERE EXISTS
(SELECT *
FROM Orders
WHERE Customers.CustomerID = Orders.CustomerID)
```

This statement returns:

Customer Name
William Smith
Natalie Lopez
Brenda Harper

Adam Petrie doesn't appear in the results since he has not placed any orders. The EXISTS keyword in the above statement is evaluated as true if the SELECT in the correlated subquery returns any data. Notice that the subquery selects all columns (SELECT *). Since it doesn't really matter what particular data is selected in the subquery, we use the asterisk to return all data. We're only interested in determining whether any data exists in the subquery.

As before, the logic in this statement can be expressed in other ways. Here's a statement that obtains the same results using a subquery with the IN operator:

```
SELECT
CustomerName AS 'Customer Name'
FROM Customers
WHERE CustomerID IN
(SELECT CustomerID
FROM Orders)
```

Here's another statement that retrieves the same data without a subquery:

```
SELECT
CustomerName AS 'Customer Name'
FROM Customers
INNER JOIN Orders
ON Customers.CustomerID = Orders.CustomerID
GROUP BY CustomerName
```

Using a Subquery as a Calculated Column

The final general use of subqueries is as a calculated column. Let's say we would like to see a list of customers, along with a count of the number of orders they have placed.

This query can actually be accomplished without subqueries with this statement:

```
SELECT
CustomerName AS 'Customer Name',
COUNT (OrderID) AS 'Number of Orders'
FROM Customers
LEFT JOIN Orders
ON Customers.CustomerID = Orders.CustomerID
GROUP BY Customers.CustomerID, CustomerName
ORDER BY Customers.CustomerID
```

The output is:

Customer Name	Number of Orders
William Smith	1
Natalie Lopez	3
Brenda Harper	2
Adam Petrie	0

However, another way of obtaining the same result is to use a subquery as a calculated column. This looks like the following:

```
SELECT
CustomerName AS 'Customer Name',
(SELECT
COUNT (OrderID)
FROM Orders
```

```
WHERE Customers.CustomerID = Orders.CustomerID)
AS 'Number of Orders'
FROM Customers
ORDER BY Customers.CustomerID
```

Notice that in this case the subquery is a correlated subquery. The subquery is used as a calculated column in the `SELECT` *columnlist*. In other words, after the subquery is evaluated, it returns a single value, which is then included in the *columnlist*. Here's a general format of the above statement:

```
SELECT
CustomerName AS 'Customer Name',
SubqueryResult AS 'Number of Orders'
FROM Customers
ORDER BY Customers.CustomerID
```

Looking Ahead

In this chapter, we've seen subqueries used in three different ways: as a data source, in selection criteria, and as a calculated column. We've also seen examples of both correlated and uncorrelated subqueries. We've really only touched on some of the uses (and abuses) of subqueries. What complicates the matter is that many subqueries can be expressed in other ways. Whether or not you choose to utilize subqueries depends on your personal taste and sometimes on the performance of the statement. In general, `SELECT` statements with subqueries tend to run more slowly than an equivalent statement without a subquery. We'll leave it to more advanced SQL books to discuss the various advantages and disadvantages of using subqueries.

Through our use of joins and subqueries, we've explored numerous ways to select data from multiple tables. In our next chapter, "Set Logic," we're going to look at a way to combine entire queries into a single SQL statement. This is a special type of logic that allows us to merge multiple data sets into a single result. As will be seen, set logic procedures are sometimes necessary in order to display sets of data that are only partially related to each other. As with subqueries, the techniques of set logic provide additional flexibility and logical possibilities for your SQL statements.

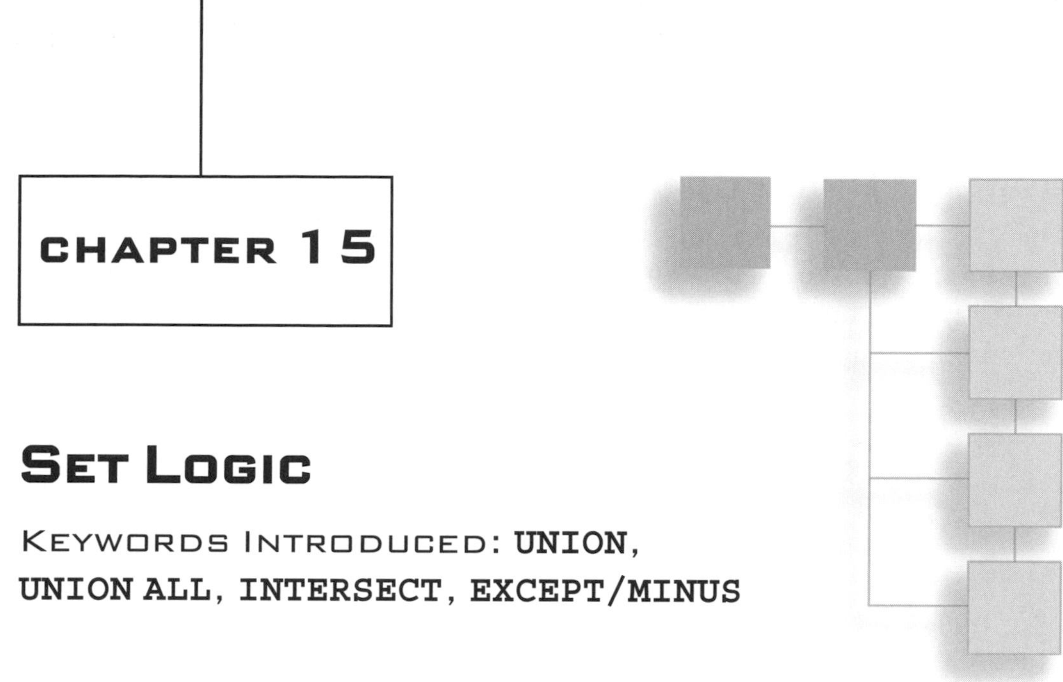

Chapter 15

Set Logic

Keywords Introduced: **UNION, UNION ALL, INTERSECT, EXCEPT/MINUS**

The various joins and subqueries of the past few chapters have dealt with different ways of combining data from multiple tables. The end result, however, has been a single `SELECT` statement. We're now going to extend the concept of combining tables to the possibility of combining data from entire queries. In other words, we're going to look at a way to write a single SQL statement that combines more than one `SELECT` to retrieve data.

The concept of combining queries is often referred to as *set logic*, a term taken from mathematics. Each `SELECT` query can be referred to as a *set* of data. The set logic we will examine in this chapter will address four scenarios. Assuming that we have data in SET A and in SET B, here are the possibilities that we want:

- Data that is in SET A or in SET B
- Data that is in both SET A and SET B
- Data that is in SET A, but not in SET B
- Data that is in SET B, but not in SET A

We're going to start with a look at the first scenario, that data is in SET A or in SET B. As will be seen, this is the most prevalent and important of the set logic possibilities.

Using the UNION Operator

The `UNION` operator in SQL is used to handle logic to select data that is either SET A or SET B. We'll start with an example. Let's say that we have two tables in our database. The first is an Orders table containing data on orders placed by customers. It might look like:

OrderID	CustomerID	OrderDate	OrderAmount
1	1	2009-10-13	10
2	2	2009-10-13	8
3	2	2009-12-05	7
4	2	2009-12-15	21
5	3	2009-12-28	11

The second table, named Returns, contains data on merchandise that has been returned by customers. It might look like:

ReturnID	CustomerID	ReturnDate	ReturnAmount
1	1	2009-10-23	2
2	2	2009-12-07	7
3	3	2009-12-28	3

It's important to note that, unlike the Refunds table seen in Chapter 12, this Returns table is not directly related to the Orders table. In other words, returns are not tied to a specific order. In this scenario, a customer might return merchandise from multiple orders.

We want to create a report of all the orders and returns from one particular customer. We would like the results sorted by either the order date if it's an order or the return date if it's a return. Here is a statement that can accomplish this. We've inserted a few extra blank lines in this statement, to emphasize the fact that it contains two completely separate `SELECT`s, combined together with the `UNION` operator:

```
SELECT
OrderDate AS 'Date',
'Order' AS 'Type',
OrderAmount AS 'Amount'
FROM Orders
WHERE CustomerID = 2

UNION

SELECT
ReturnDate AS 'Date',
'Return' AS 'Type',
ReturnAmount AS 'Amount'
FROM Returns
WHERE CustomerID = 2

ORDER BY Date
```

The resulting date is:

Date	Type	Amount
2009-10-13	Order	8
2009-12-05	Order	7
2009-12-07	Return	7
2009-12-15	Order	21

As seen, the `UNION` operator separates two completely separate `SELECT` statements. There is also an `ORDER BY` clause at the very end, which applies to the results of both `SELECT` statements. The general format for the previous statement is:

```
SelectStatementOne
UNION
SelectStatementTwo
ORDER BY columnlist
```

In order for the `UNION` to work, three rules must be followed:

- All `SELECT` statements combined together with a `UNION` must have the same number of columns in the `SELECT` *columnlist*.
- All columns in each `SELECT` *columnlist* must be in the same order.

- All corresponding columns in each SELECT *columnlist* must have the same, or compatible, datatypes.

With reference to these rules, notice that both SELECT statements in the search have three columns. Each of the three columns has data in the same order and with the same datatype.

When using the UNION, you should use column aliases to give the same column name to all corresponding columns. In our example, the first column of the first SELECT has an original name of OrderDate. The first column of the second SELECT has an original name of ReturnDate. To ensure that the first column in the final result has the desired name, both OrderDate and ReturnDate are given a column alias of Date. This also allows the column to be referenced in an ORDER BY *columnlist*.

Also notice that the second column of each SELECT utilizes literal values. We created a calculated column named Type, which has a value of either Order or Return. This allows us to tell which table each row comes from.

Finally, notice that the ORDER BY clause applies to the final results of both queries combined together. This is how it should be, since there would be no point to applying a sort to the individual queries.

At this point, it is useful to step back and talk about why it was necessary to employ the UNION operator rather than simply join the Orders and Returns tables together in a single SELECT statement. Since both tables have a CustomerID column, why didn't we simply join the two tables together on this column? The problem with this possibility is that the two tables are really only indirectly related to each. Customers can place orders and customers can initiate returns, but there is no direct connection between orders and returns.

Additionally, even if there were a direct connection between the two tables, a join would not accomplish what is desired. With a proper join, related information can be placed together on the same row. In this case, however, we are interested in showing orders and returns on separate rows. The UNION operator must be used to display data in this manner.

In essence, the UNION allows us to retrieve unrelated or partially related data in a single statement.

Distinct and Non-Distinct Unions

There are actually two variations of the UNION operator: UNION and UNION ALL. There is only a slight difference between the two. The UNION operator eliminates all duplicate rows. The UNION ALL operator specifies that all rows are to be included, even if they are duplicates.

The UNION operator eliminates duplicates in a manner similar to the DISTINCT keyword previously seen. Whereas DISTINCT applies to a single SELECT, the UNION eliminates duplicates in all SELECT statements combined together via the UNION.

In the previous example with the Orders and Returns tables, there was no possibility of duplication, so it didn't matter which was used. Here's an example that illustrates the difference. Let's say that you are only interested in the dates on which any orders or returns were issued. You don't want to see multiple rows for the same date. The following statement accomplishes this task:

```
SELECT
OrderDate AS 'Date'
FROM Orders
UNION
SELECT
ReturnDate AS 'Date'
FROM Returns
Order by Date
```

The resulting data is:

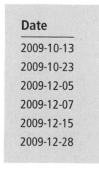

Date
2009-10-13
2009-10-23
2009-12-05
2009-12-07
2009-12-15
2009-12-28

Notice that there is only one occurrence of 2009-12-28. Even though there is one row with 2009-12-28 in the Orders table and one row with 2009-12-28 in the Returns table, the UNION operator ensures that the 2009-12-28 date is only listed once.

Let's change the statement, adding a DISTINCT to each individual SELECT, but also specifying UNION ALL rather than UNION, as follows:

```
SELECT
DISTINCT
OrderDate AS 'Date'
FROM Orders
UNION ALL
SELECT
DISTINCT
ReturnDate AS 'Date'
FROM Returns
ORDER BY Date
```

The output is now:

Date
2009-10-13
2009-10-23
2009-12-05
2009-12-07
2009-12-15
2009-12-28
2009-12-28

The DISTINCT ensures that each order date or return date is only listed once. Even though there are two orders from 2009-10-13, that date is only shown one time. However, the UNION ALL allows duplicates between the Orders SELECT and the Returns SELECT. So you can see that 2009-12-28 is listed twice, once from the Orders table and once from the Returns table.

Intersecting Queries

The UNION and UNION ALL operators return data that is in either of the sets specified in the two SELECT statements being combined. This is like using an OR operator to combine data from two logical sets.

SQL provides an operator called INTERSECT, which only pulls data that is in both of the two sets being looked at. The INTERSECT is analogous to the AND operator and handles the second scenario stated at the start of the chapter:

- Data that is in both SET A and SET B

DATABASE DIFFERENCES: MySQL

MySQL doesn't support the `INTERSECT` operator.

Using the same Orders and Returns tables, let's say that you want to see dates on which there are both orders and returns. A statement that accomplishes this is:

```
SELECT
OrderDate AS 'Date'
FROM Orders
INTERSECT
SELECT
ReturnDate AS 'Date'
FROM Returns
ORDER BY Date
```

The result is:

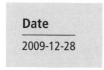

Date
2009-12-28

Only one row is shown because this is the only date that appears in both the Orders and Returns tables.

There is one additional variation on the intersect operation, which is provided by the `EXCEPT` operator. Whereas the `INTERSECT` returns data that is in both sets, the `EXCEPT` returns data that is in one set but not the other and handles the third and fourth scenarios stated at the start of the chapter:

- Data that is in SET A, but not in SET B
- Data that is in SET B, but not in SET A

The general format of the `EXCEPT` is:

```
SelectStatementOne
EXCEPT
SelectStatementTwo
ORDER BY columnlist
```

This statement will show data that is in *SelectStatementOne* but not in *Select-StatementTwo*. Here's an example:

```
SELECT
OrderDate AS 'Date'
FROM Orders
EXCEPT
SELECT
ReturnDate AS 'Date'
FROM Returns
ORDER BY Date
```

The result is:

Date
2009-10-13
2009-12-05
2009-12-15

This data shows dates on which orders were placed, but on which no refunds were issued. Notice that 2009-12-28 does not appear, since a refund was issued on that date.

DATABASE DIFFERENCES: MySQL and Oracle

MySQL doesn't support the `EXCEPT` operator.

The equivalent of the `EXCEPT` operator in Oracle is `MINUS`.

Looking Ahead

In this chapter, we've seen different ways to combine multiple sets of `SELECT` statements into a single statement. The most commonly used operator is the `UNION`, which allows you to combine data that is in either of two different sets. The `UNION` is analogous to the `OR` operator. The `UNION ALL` is a variant of the `UNION` that allows duplicate rows to be shown. Similarly, the `INTERCEPT` operator allows that data to be presented if it is in both of the two sets of data being combined. The `INTERCEPT` is analogous to the `AND` operator. Finally, the `EXCEPT` operator allows for selection of data that is in one set but not in another.

Our next chapter, "Stored Procedures and Parameters," will relate how you can save multiple SQL statements in a procedure and make use of parameters in those procedures to add a degree of generality to your SQL commands. We'll also talk about the possibility of creating your own custom functions and explain how functions differ from stored procedures. Much like the views discussed in Chapter 13, stored procedures and custom functions are useful objects that you can create and store in your database to provide some extra polish and functionality for your systems.

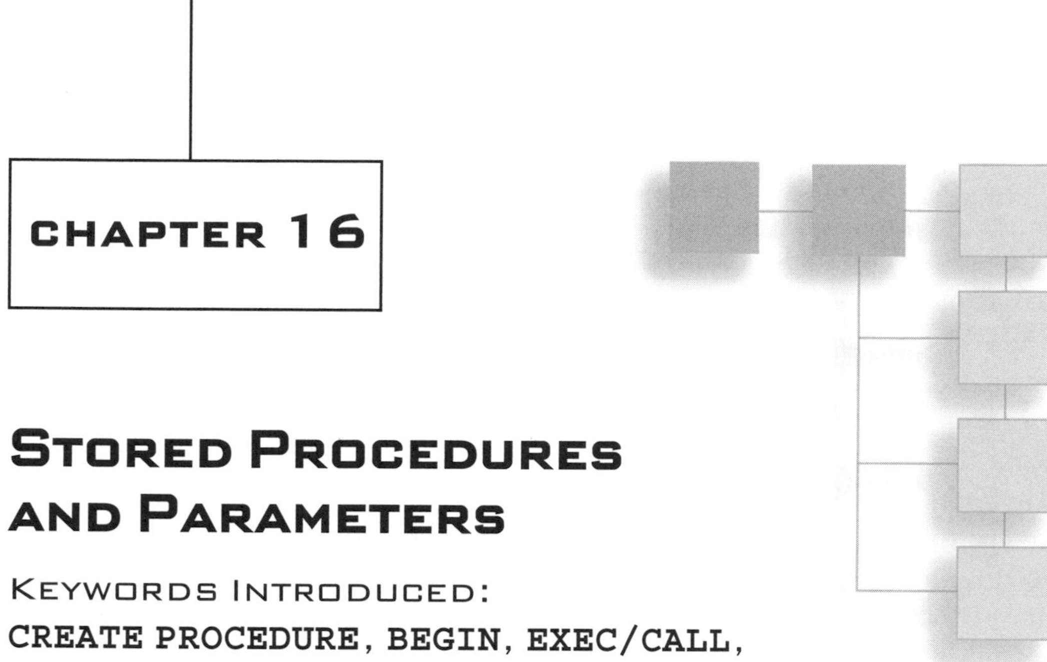

Chapter 16

Stored Procedures and Parameters

Keywords Introduced:

CREATE PROCEDURE, BEGIN, EXEC/CALL, ALTER PROCEDURE, DROP PROCEDURE

Up until now, all of our data retrieval has been accomplished with a single statement. Even the set logic seen in the previous chapter was accomplished by combining multiple SELECTs into a single statement. We're now going to discuss a new scenario in which multiple statements can be saved into a single object known as a *stored procedure.*

In broad terms, there are two general reasons why you might want to use stored procedures:

- To save multiple SQL statements in a single procedure
- To use parameters in conjunction with your SQL statements

Stored procedures can, in fact, consist of a single SQL statement and contain no parameters. But the real value of stored procedures becomes evident when they contain multiple statements or parameters.

The subject of stored procedures is quite complex. In this brief review of the subject, we'll focus on an overview of the second stated reason—that of using parameters in stored procedures. This is something that relates directly to the issue of how to best retrieve data from a database. As you'll see, the ability to add parameters to a SELECT statement turns out to be a very useful feature in everyday use.

The use of stored procedures to contain multiple statements is beyond the scope of this book. Basically, the ability to store multiple statements in a procedure means that you can create complex logic and execute it all at once as a single transaction. For example, you might have a business requirement to take an incoming order from a customer and quickly evaluate it before accepting it from the customer. This procedure might involve checking to make sure that the items are in stock, verifying that the customer haa a good credit rating, and getting an initial estimate as to when it can be shipped. This situation would require multiple SQL statements with some added logic to determine what kind of message to return if all were not well with the order. All of that logic could be placed into a single stored procedure, which would enhance the modularity of the system. With everything in one procedure, that logic could be executed from any calling program, and it would always return the same result.

Creating Stored Procedures

Before we get into the details of how to utilize stored procedures, let's cover the mechanics of how they are created and maintained. The syntax varies significantly among different databases.

The general format for creating a stored procedure in Microsoft SQL Server is:

```
CREATE PROCEDURE ProcedureName
AS
OptionalParameterDeclarations
BEGIN
SQLStatements
END
```

The CREATE PROCEDURE keyword allows you to issue a single command that creates the procedure. The procedure itself can contain any number of SQL statements and can also contain parameter declarations. We'll talk about the parameter declaration syntax later. The SQL statements are listed between BEGIN and END keywords.

DATABASE DIFFERENCES: MySQL and Oracle

The general format for creating a stored procedure in MySQL is slightly more complex. The format is:

```
DELIMITER $$
CREATE PROCEDURE ProcedureName ()
BEGIN
SQLStatements
END$$
DELIMITER ;
```

MySQL requires delimiters when executing multiple statements. The normal delimiter is a semicolon. The first line in the above code temporarily changes the delimiter from a semicolon to two dollar signs. Any needed parameters are specified between the parentheses on the `CREATE PROCEDURE` line. Then each SQL statement listed between the `BEGIN` and `END` keywords must have a semicolon at the end of the statement. The dollars signs are written after the `END` keyword to denote that the `CREATE PROCEDURE` command is completed. Finally, another `DELIMITER` statement is placed at the end to change the delimiter back to a semicolon.

The procedure for creating stored procedures in Oracle is quite a bit more involved and is beyond the scope of this book. In order to create a stored procedure for a `SELECT` statement in Oracle, you will need to first create an object called a *package*. The package will contain two basic components: a *specification* and a *body*. The specification component specifies how to communicate with the body component. The body component contains the SQL statements, which are at the heart of the stored procedure.

Here's an example of how to create a stored procedure that can be used to execute this single `SELECT` statement:

```
SELECT *
FROM Customers
```

The procedure will be named ProcedureOne. In Microsoft SQL Server, the statement to create the procedure is:

```
CREATE PROCEDURE ProcedureOne
AS
BEGIN
SELECT *
FROM Customers
END
```

DATABASE DIFFERENCES: MySQL

In MySQL, the previous example would look like:

```
DELIMITER $$
CREATE PROCEDURE ProcedureOne ()
BEGIN
SELECT *
FROM Customers;
END$$
DELIMITER ;
```

Remember that creating a stored procedure does not execute anything. It simply creates the procedure so that it can be executed later. Along with tables and views, the procedure will be visible in your database management tool so that you can view its contents.

Parameters in Stored Procedures

All of the SELECT statements you have seen up until now have had a certain static quality due to the fact that they were written to retrieve data in one specific way. The ability to add parameters to SELECT statements gives you the possibility of much greater flexibility.

The term *parameter* in SQL statements is similar to the term *variable*, as it is used in other computer languages. A parameter is basically a value that is passed to a SQL statement by the calling program. It can have whatever value the user specifies at the time the call is made.

Let's start with a simple example. We have a SELECT statement that retrieves data from a Customers table. Rather than select all customers, we would like the SELECT to retrieve data for only one specific CustomerID number. However, we don't want to code the number directly in the SELECT statement. We want the SELECT statement to be general enough so it can accept any provided CustomerID number and then execute with that value. The SELECT statement without any parameters is simply:

```
SELECT *
FROM Customers
```

Our goal is to add a WHERE clause that will allow us to select data for a particular customer. In a general form, we'd like the SELECT statement to be:

```
SELECT *
FROM Customers
WHERE CustomerID = ParameterValue
```

In Microsoft SQL Server, the creation of such a stored procedure can be accomplished with:

```
CREATE PROCEDURE CustomerProcedure
(@CustID INT)
AS
BEGIN
SELECT *
FROM Customers
WHERE CustomerID = @CustID
END
```

Notice the addition of the second line, which specifies the CustID parameter in the procedure. In Microsoft SQL Server, the @ symbol is used to denote a parameter. The INT keyword is placed after the parameter to indicate that this parameter will have an integer value. The same parameter name is used in the WHERE clause.

DATABASE DIFFERENCES: MySQL

In MySQL, the command to create an equivalent stored procedure is:

```
DELIMITER $$
CREATE PROCEDURE CustomerProcedure
(CustID INT)
BEGIN
SELECT *
FROM Customers
WHERE CustomerID = CustID;
END$$
DELIMITER ;
```

Notice that MySQL doesn't require the @ symbol to denote a parameter.

When a stored procedure is executed, the calling program passes a value for the parameter, and the SQL statement is executed as if that value were part of the statement.

It should also be noted that the parameters discussed previously are input parameters. As such, they contain values that passed into the stored procedure. Stored procedures can also include output parameters, which can contain values passed back to the calling program. It's beyond the scope of this book to discuss the various nuances of how to specify both input and output parameters in stored procedures.

Executing Stored Procedures

After stored procedures are created, how are they executed? The syntax varies between databases. Microsoft SQL Server provides the `EXEC` keyword to run stored procedures.

In Microsoft SQL Server, the following statement will execute the ProcedureOne procedure:

```
EXEC ProcedureOne
```

When this statement is executed, it brings back the results of the `SELECT` statement contained in the stored procedure.

The ProcedureOne procedure didn't have any parameters, so the syntax is simple. How do you execute procedures with input parameters? The following executes the CustomerProcedure procedure for a CustID value of 2:

```
EXEC CustomerProcedure
@CustID = 2
```

DATABASE DIFFERENCES: MySQL

Rather than using `EXEC`, MySQL uses a `CALL` keyword to execute stored procedures, and the syntax for stored procedures with parameters is slightly different. The equivalent of the previous two `EXEC` statements in MySQL is:

```
CALL ProcedureOne;
CALL CustomerProcedure (2);
```

Modifying and Deleting Stored Procedures

Once a stored procedure is created, it can be modified. Just as the ALTER VIEW keyword was used to modify views, the ALTER PROCEDURE keyword is used to modify stored procedures. The syntax is identical to the CREATE PROCEDURE, except that the word ALTER is used in place of CREATE. Just as the CREATE PROCEDURE has a slightly different syntax for each database, so does the ALTER PROCEDURE.

You've already seen this example of creating a stored procedure with Microsoft SQL Server:

```
CREATE PROCEDURE CustomerProcedure
(@CustID INT)
AS
BEGIN
SELECT *
FROM Customers
WHERE CustomerID = @CustID
END
```

After this procedure is created, if you wanted to alter the procedure to select only the top five rows from the Customers table, the command to accomplish that would be:

```
ALTER PROCEDURE CustomerProcedure
(@CustID INT)
AS
BEGIN
SELECT
TOP 5 *
FROM Customers
WHERE CustomerID = @CustID
END
```

DATABASE DIFFERENCES: MySQL

MySQL provides an ALTER PROCEDURE command, but it has limited functionality. To alter the content of a stored procedure in MySQL, you need to issue a DROP PROCEDURE and then a CREATE PROCEDURE with the new content.

Deleting a stored procedure is even simpler. Just as the DROP VIEW deletes a view, the DROP PROCEDURE statement deletes a procedure.

Here's how the stored procedure named CustomerProcedure can be deleted:

```
DROP PROCEDURE CustomerProcedure
```

Functions Revisited

In Chapter 4, we talked about the built-in scalar functions that are available in SQL. For example, we used character functions such as `LEFT` and mathematical functions such as `ROUND`. In Chapter 10, we discussed aggregate functions such as `MAX`.

In addition to the built-in functions in SQL, developers can create their own functions and save them in a database. The procedure for creating functions is very similar to the procedure for creating stored procedures. SQL provides the keywords `CREATE FUNCTION`, `ALTER FUNCTION`, and `DROP FUNCTION`, which work very much like `CREATE PROCEDURE`, `ALTER PROCEDURE`, and `DROP PROCEDURE`.

Due to the advanced nature of this topic, we're not going to provide specific examples of this functionality. However, we'll spend a few moments explaining the differences between using stored procedures and functions.

Both stored procedures and functions can be saved in a database. These entities are saved as separate objects in a database, much like tables or views. The procedures for saving and modifying stored procedures and functions are very similar. The same `CREATE`, `ALTER`, and `DROP` commands for stored procedures can be used for functions.

The difference between the two lies in how they are used and in their capabilities. There are two main distinctions between stored procedures and functions:

- **Stored procedures can have any number of output parameters.** They can even have zero output parameters. In contrast, a function must always contain exactly one output parameter. In other words, when you call a function, you always get back a single value.
- **Stored procedures are executed by a calling program.** The stored procedure cannot be directly referenced in a `SELECT` statement. In contrast, functions can be referenced within statements, as seen in Chapters 4 and 10. After you define your own function, you'll reference that function by the name you specified when the function was created.

Looking Ahead

In this chapter, we've seen that the use of parameters can add a great deal of flexibility to the process of retrieving data. For example, parameters allow you to generalize SQL statements so that values for selection criteria can be specified at the time the statement is executed. You've also learned the basics of how to create and modify stored procedures. Finally, we explained some of the differences between stored procedures and user-defined functions.

Although the examples in the present chapter were focused on data retrieval, stored procedures and functions are also quite useful in applying data updates. Our next chapter, "Modifying Data," will take us completely out of the realm of data retrieval and move us squarely into issues surrounding the need to update data. The business of maintaining data doesn't present the same analytic possibilities as data retrieval, but it is a necessary task for any enterprise. Fortunately, most of the techniques you've learned with the `SELECT` statement apply equally to the modification processes to be discussed in the next chapter.

Chapter 17

Modifying Data

Keywords Introduced: **INSERT INTO, VALUES, DELETE, TRUNCATE TABLE, UPDATE**

Having exhausted our discussion of retrieving data from databases, we will now move on to the topic of how to modify data. There are three basic scenarios as to how data can be modified:

- Inserting new rows into a table
- Deleting rows from a table
- Updating existing data in specific rows and columns in a table

As you may surmise, inserting and deleting rows is relatively straightforward. Updating existing data, however, is a more complex endeavor. We'll begin with the insert and delete functions and then conclude with updates.

Modification Strategies

The mechanics of modifying data are fairly straightforward. However, the nature of the process means that this is an area fraught with danger. Being human, mistakes can be made. With a single command, you can easily delete thousands of rows in error. Or you can apply numerous updates that may be difficult to retract.

As a practical matter, there are various strategies that can be employed to help prevent catastrophic blunders. For example, when deleting rows from a table, you can employ a *soft delete* technique, which means that instead of actually deleting rows, you can denote a special column in a table that marks each row as either active or inactive. Rather than deleting a row, you merely mark a row as being inactive. That way, if a delete is done in error, you can easily reverse it by changing the value of the active/inactive column.

A similar technique can be utilized when doing inserts. When adding a row, you can mark in a special column the exact date and time of the insert. If it is later determined that the row was added in error, you can find all rows added in a specified time range and have them deleted.

The problem is more complex when it comes to updating data. Generally, it's advisable to maintain a separate table that holds data on intended update transactions. If any kind of error is made, you can go back to the transaction table to look up the before-and-after values for data that was modified and use that to reverse any earlier mistakes.

The above mentioned strategies are just a few of the many approaches that can be taken. This is a topic that is well beyond the scope of this book. Just be sure that you are very cautious when updating data. Unlike many user-friendly desktop applications, there is no undo command in SQL.

Inserting Data

SQL provides an `INSERT` keyword to add data into a table. There are two basic ways in which an `INSERT` can be done:

- Insert specific data that is listed in an `INSERT` statement
- Insert data that is obtained from a `SELECT` statement

Let's start with an example that shows how to insert data, where the data values are specified in the `INSERT` statement. Let's assume that we have a Customers table with this data already in it:

CustomerID	FirstName	LastName	State
1	William	Smith	IL
2	Natalie	Lopez	WI
3	Brenda	Harper	NV

Let's also assume that the first column, CustomerID, is the primary key for the table. Back in Chapters 1 and 2, we talked about the fact that primary keys enforce the requirement that each row in a table should be uniquely identifiable. We also mentioned that it is often the case that primary key columns are specified as auto-increment columns. This means that they are automatically assigned a number as a row is added to the table.

Assuming that the CustomerID column is defined as an auto-increment column, this means that when we add a row to the Customers table, we don't specify a value for the CustomerID column. It will be automatically determined as a row is added to the table. We only need to specify values for the other three columns.

Let's proceed with an attempt to add two new customers to the table: Virginia Jones from Ohio and Clark Woodland from California.

This statement performs the insert:

```
INSERT INTO Customers
(FirstName, LastName, State)
VALUES
('Virginia', 'Jones', 'OH'),
('Clark', 'Woodland', 'CA')
```

After the insert, the table contains:

CustomerID	FirstName	LastName	State
1	William	Smith	IL
2	Natalie	Lopez	WI
3	Brenda	Harper	NV
4	Virginia	Jones	OH
5	Clark	Woodland	CA

A few words of explanation are in order. First, notice that the `VALUES` keyword is used as a prefix to lists of values to be inserted into the table. The statement lists each row of data in a separate set of parentheses. Virginia Jones of Ohio was in one set of parentheses; Clark Woodland was in another set. The two sets were separated by a comma. If we needed to only add one row, then just one set of parentheses would be needed.

DATABASE DIFFERENCES: Oracle

Oracle doesn't permit multiple rows to be specified after the `VALUES` keyword. The previous example would need to be broken down into two statements, such as:

```
INSERT INTO Customers
(FirstName, LastName, State)
VALUES ('Virginia', 'Jones', 'OH');

INSERT INTO Customers
(FirstName, LastName, State)
VALUES ('Clark', 'Woodland', 'CA');
```

Also note that the order of values after the `VALUES` keyword corresponds to the order of columns listed in the *columnlist* after the `INSERT TO`. The order in which the columns are listed does not have to be the same as it is in the database. In other words, the above insert just as easily could have been accomplished with this statement:

```
INSERT INTO Customers
(State, LastName, FirstName)
VALUES
('OH', 'Jones', 'Virginia'),
('CA', 'Woodland', 'Clark')
```

In the above `INSERT`, we listed the State column first instead of last. Again, the order in which columns are listed doesn't matter.

To sum up, the general format for the `INSERT INTO` statement is:

```
INSERT INTO table
(columnlist)
VALUES
(RowValues1),
(RowValues2)
(repeat any number of times)
```

The columns in *columnlist* need to correspond to the columns in *RowValues.*

Also, if all the columns in *columnlist* are listed in the same order as they physically exist in the database, and if there are no auto-increment columns in the table, then the INSERT INTO statement can be executed without specifying the *columnlist.* However, this practice is strongly discouraged since it is prone to error.

What happens when not all columns are specified in an INSERT? Simple. Those columns that are not specified are given NULL values. For example, let's say we want to insert one additional row into the Customers table, for a customer named Tom Monroe. However, we don't know Tom's state. Here's the INSERT:

```
INSERT INTO Customers
(FirstName, LastName)
VALUES
('Tom', 'Monroe')
```

Afterwards, his row in the table appears as:

CustomerID	FirstName	LastName	State
6	Tom	Monroe	NULL

Since we didn't specify a value for the State column for this new row, it is given a NULL value.

There are two variations of the INSERT INTO statement. The second format applies to situations where you insert data that is obtained from a SELECT statement, which means that instead of listing values after a VALUES keyword, you substitute a SELECT statement that obtains similar values.

Let's say that we have another table named CustomerTransactions, which holds data that we would like to insert into the Customers table. The Customer-Transactions table might look like:

CustomerID	State	Name1	Name2
1	RI	Susan	Harris
2	DC	Michael	Blake
3	RI	Alan	Canter

If we wanted to add all customers in the state of Rhode Island from the CustomerTransactions table to the Customers table, the following would accomplish that objective:

```
INSERT INTO Customers
(FirstName, LastName, State)
SELECT
Name1,
Name2,
State
FROM CustomerTransactions
WHERE State = 'RI'
```

After this `INSERT`, the Customers table contains:

CustomerID	FirstName	LastName	State
1	William	Smith	IL
2	Natalie	Lopez	WI
3	Brenda	Harper	NV
4	Virginia	Jones	OH
5	Clark	Woodland	CA
6	Tom	Monroe	NULL
7	Susan	Harris	RI
8	Alan	Canter	RI

The above `INSERT` simply substituted a `SELECT` statement for the previously seen `VALUES` clause. As would be expected, Michael Blake didn't get added to the Customers table, since he is not in Rhode Island. Also notice that the column names in the Customers and CustomerTransactions tables are not identical. The column names don't matter as long as the columns are listed in the correct corresponding order.

Deleting Data

Deleting data is much simpler than adding it. The `DELETE` statement is used to handle deletes. When a `DELETE` is executed, it deletes entire rows, not individual columns in a row. The general format is:

```
DELETE
FROM table
WHERE condition
```

Here's a simple example. Let's say we want to delete rows from the previously mentioned Customers table if the customer is in Rhode Island. The statement to accomplish this is:

```
DELETE
FROM Customers
WHERE State = 'RI'
```

That's all there is to it. If you wanted to test the results of the above `DELETE` before executing it, you would simply substitute a `SELECT` for `DELETE`, as follows:

```
SELECT
COUNT (*)
FROM Customers
WHERE State = 'RI'
```

This would provide a count of the rows to be deleted, which supplies some level of validation for the delete.

There is one other option for deleting data that is worth mentioning. If you want to delete all the data in a single table, you can employ a `TRUNCATE TABLE` statement to delete everything. The advantage of the `TRUNCATE TABLE` over the `DELETE` statement is that it is much faster. Unlike the `DELETE`, the `TRUNCATE TABLE` doesn't log the results of the transaction. We haven't talked about database log processes, but this is a function that most databases provide that allows database administrators to recover databases in the event of system crashes and other similar problems.

If you want to delete all rows in the Customers table, you can issue this statement:

```
TRUNCATE TABLE Customers
```

This has the same result as this statement:

```
DELETE
FROM Customers
```

One other slight difference between `DELETE` and `TRUNCATE TABLE` is that TRUNCATE TABLE resets the current values used for auto-increment columns. The `DELETE` doesn't affect those values.

Updating Data

The procedure for updating data involves specifying which columns are to be updated, as well as logic for selecting rows. The general format for an UPDATE statement is:

```
UPDATE table
SET Column1 = Expression1,
Column2 = Expression2
(repeat any number of times)
WHERE condition
```

This statement is similar to the basic SELECT, except that the SET keyword is used to assign new values to specified columns. The WHERE condition specifies which rows are to be updated, but the UPDATE statement can update multiple columns at the same time. If more than one column is being updated, the SET keyword is only listed once, but a comma must separate all update expressions.

Starting with a simple example, let's say we want to change the name of customer William Smith to Bill Smythe. His row in the Customers table currently looks like:

CustomerID	FirstName	LastName	State
1	William	Smith	IL

The UPDATE statement to accomplish the change is:

```
UPDATE Customers
SET FirstName = 'Bill',
LastName = 'Smythe'
WHERE CustomerID = 1
```

After executing this statement, this row in the Customers table appears as:

CustomerID	FirstName	LastName	State
1	Bill	Smythe	IL

Notice that the value of the State column is unchanged since that column was not included in the UPDATE statement. Also note that the WHERE clause is essential. Without the WHERE clause, every row in the table would have been changed to Bill Smythe.

Correlated Subquery Updates

The previous UPDATE example is easy enough but not entirely realistic. A more common example of an UPDATE involves situations where you update data in one table based on data in another table. Let's say we have this Customers table:

CustomerID	State	Zip
1	IL	60089
2	CA	92802
3	WI	53718
4	DC	20024
5	FL	32801

This CustomerTransactions table has the recent changes for existing customers:

TransactionID	CustomerID	State	Zip
1	1	IL	60090
2	2	NV	89109
3	5	FL	32810

The Customers table is considered to be the main source of data for customers. In order to accomplish an update of the Customers table from the CustomerTransactions table, we're going to need to use the correlated subquery technique discussed in Chapter 14. The correlated subquery is needed because the UPDATE statement can only specify a single table to update. We can't merely join multiple tables together and have it work. We'll need to use a correlated subquery after the SET keyword to indicate where the data comes from.

The following statement can be utilized to update the State and Zip columns in the Customers table from the transactions in the CustomerTransactions table. Since this statement is fairly complex, we've inserted a few blank lines so we can subsequently discuss the four sections of the statement.

```
UPDATE Customers

SET Customers.State =
(SELECT CustomerTransactions.State
FROM CustomerTransactions
WHERE CustomerTransactions.CustomerID = Customers.CustomerID),

Customers.Zip =
(SELECT CustomerTransactions.Zip
FROM CustomerTransactions
WHERE CustomerTransactions.CustomerID = Customers.CustomerID)

WHERE EXISTS
(SELECT *
FROM CustomerTransactions
WHERE CustomerTransactions.CustomerID = Customers.CustomerID)
```

After executing this `UPDATE`, the Customers table contains:

CustomerID	State	Zip
1	IL	60090
2	NV	89109
3	WI	53562
4	MD	20814
5	FL	32810

Let's analyze this `UPDATE` statement in some detail. The first section of the statement, consisting of the first line, indicates that the update is to be done on the Customers table.

The second section of the statement specifies how the State column is to be updated. The update is based on this correlated subquery:

```
SELECT CustomerTransactions.State
FROM CustomerTransactions
WHERE CustomerTransactions.CustomerID =
Customers.CustomerID
```

We can tell that this is a correlated subquery because it would error if we attempted to execute this `SELECT` on its own. The subquery is taking data from the CustomerTransactions table and matching between the two tables by CustomerID.

The third section of the statement is identical to the second section, except that these lines are concerned with updates to the Zip column. Also notice that the `SET` keyword only needed to be specified once, in the second section. It isn't needed in the third section.

The final section has logic in a `WHERE` clause associated with the selection logic for the entire `UPDATE` statement. The `EXISTS` operator is used along with another correlated subquery to determine whether rows exist in the CustomerTransactions table for each CustomerID in the Customers table. Without this `WHERE` clause, the update would incorrectly change the State and Zip columns for customers 3 and 4 to NULL values because these customers do not have rows in the CustomerTransactions table. The correlated subquery in this `WHERE` clause makes certain that we only apply updates for customers who do, in fact, have data in the CustomerTransactions table.

As can be inferred, the subject of using correlated subqueries for updates is quite complex. As such, the topic is generally beyond the scope of this book. However, we've included this example if only to give an idea of some of the complexities that are involved in data updates. Additionally, it should be noted that correlated subqueries are similarly useful with deletes.

Looking Ahead

This chapter presented an overview of the various methods of updating data. The mechanics of executing simple inserts, deletes, and updates are relatively straightforward. However, the correlated subquery technique, which is often necessary for real-world updates and deletes, is not for the faint of heart. Additionally, the entire notion of applying updates to data is a demanding exercise. With the power of SQL's ability to update thousands of rows of data with a single command comes an admonition to be cautious when performing any type of update. Procedures for reversing any updates should be carefully planned out before any data modifications are applied.

Now that we've talked about modifying the data in tables, we next progress to a discussion of the tables themselves. In the next chapter, "Maintaining Tables," we're going to look at the mechanics of creating tables along with all the attributes needed to properly hold the data in those tables. As such, we'll be revisiting some of the topics touched upon in Chapter 1, such as primary and foreign keys, in greater detail. Up until now, we've assumed that tables are simply available for our use. After this examination, you'll have a much better idea of how to create the tables that will hold your data.

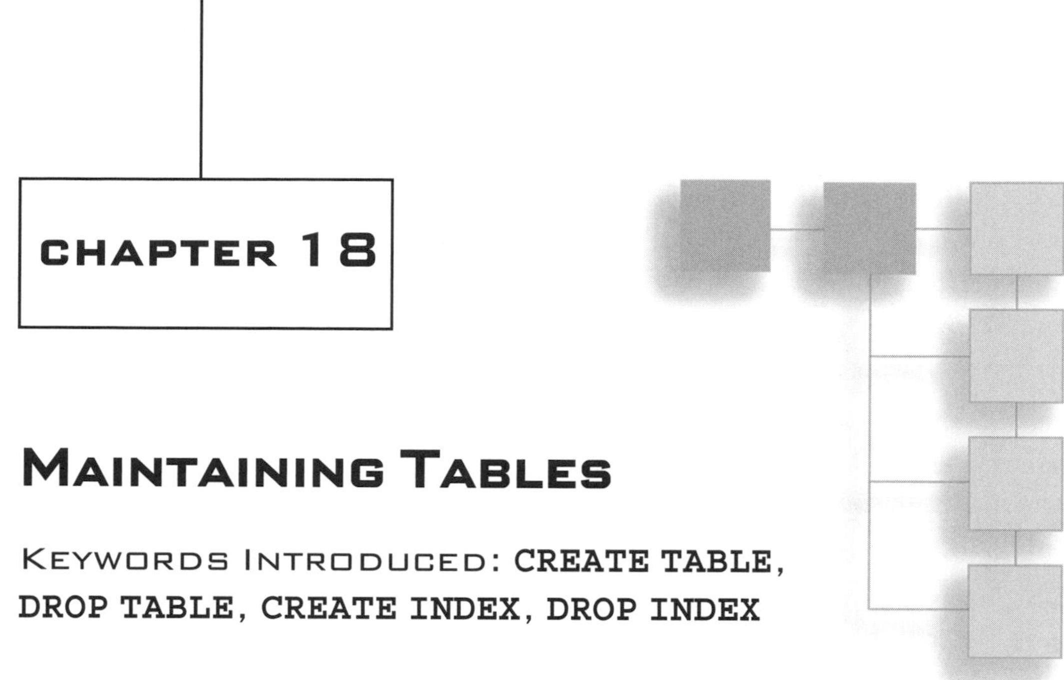

Chapter 18

Maintaining Tables

Keywords Introduced: **CREATE TABLE, DROP TABLE, CREATE INDEX, DROP INDEX**

With this chapter, we change our focus from data retrieval and modification to design. Up until now, we've assumed that tables simply exist and are available to us. However, in the normal course of events, you need to create tables before the data in them can be accessed. We now turn to the question of how to create and maintain tables.

We've previously touched on a few of the topics we'll be addressing, such as primary and foreign keys, but we now want to delve into these areas in greater detail and also bring in the related topic of table indexes.

Data Definition Language

Way back in Chapter 1, we mentioned that there are three main components of the SQL language: DML (Data Manipulation Language), DDL (Data Definition Language), and DCL (Data Control Language). Up until now, most of what we've talked about has been DML. DML statements allow you to manipulate data in relational databases by retrieval, insertion, deletion, or update. This is handled by the `SELECT`, `INSERT`, `DELETE`, and `UPDATE` statements.

Although our focus has been on DML, we have already seen a few instances of DDL (Data Definition Language). The `CREATE VIEW` and `CREATE PROCEDURE` statements are DDL, and so are the related `ALTER` and `DROP` versions of those statements.

The CREATE VIEW and CREATE PROCEDURE statements are DDL because they only allow you to manipulate the database itself. They have nothing to do with the data in databases.

In this chapter, we're going to give a brief overview of a few additional DDL statements, which can be utilized to create and modify tables and indexes.

Each database has a different way of organizing its objects, and therefore has different available DDL statements. For example, MySQL has 11 different CREATE statements for these types of objects: Databases, Events, Functions, Indexes, Logfile Groups, Procedures, Servers, Tables, TableSpaces, Triggers, and Views.

Oracle has over 30 different CREATE commands for the object types in its database. Microsoft SQL Server has over 40 different CREATE commands for its object types.

In truth, most modifications to database objects, such as views and tables, can be accomplished through the visual GUI (graphical user interface), which each software vendor provides to administer their software. It is often not necessary to learn any DDL at all, since it can usually be handled with the software GUI.

However, it's useful at least to be aware of the existence of a few key statements to manipulate data objects. We've already seen some statements that allow us to modify views and stored procedures. In this chapter, we'll show you some of the possibilities for modifying tables and indexes via DDL.

Table Attributes

In Chapter 1, we briefly discussed a few attributes of database tables, such as primary keys, foreign keys, and datatypes. In Chapter 2, we extended that discussion to talk about auto-increment columns.

As mentioned, SQL DDL provides CREATE statements for many types of database objects. In Chapter 13, we talked about the CREATE PROCEDURE and CREATE VIEW statements that handle stored procedures and views.

We're now going to bring our attention back to tables. Tables are perhaps the primary and most essential object type in a database. Without tables, nothing else really matters. All the data in a database is physically stored in tables. Most other object types relate to tables in one way or another. Views provide a virtual view of tables. Stored procedures generally act upon data in tables. Functions allow for special rules for the manipulation of data in tables.

We'll focus here on how tables can be created initially. There are a large number of attributes that can be associated with table definitions. We're going to give an overview of some of the more important attributes and discuss what they mean.

The subject of table attributes is also related to the larger topic of database design, which will be addressed in the next chapter. For now, we want to focus on the mechanics of what can be done with the tables themselves.

The specifics of how tables can be designed and altered varies widely among Microsoft SQL Server, MySQL, and Oracle. We'll talk primarily about those attributes that are common to tables in all three databases.

Table Columns

Tables are defined as containing any number of columns. Each column has a number of attributes specific to that column. The first and most obvious attribute is the column name. Each column must be given a name unique to that table.

A second attribute of columns is the datatype, a subject that was addressed in Chapter 1. We've already described some notable datatypes in three main categories: numeric, character, and date/time. The datatype is a key determinant of what type of data each column can contain.

A third attribute of columns is whether or not it can be defined as an auto-increment column. We briefly introduced this attribute type in Chapter 2 and talked about it further in the previous chapter about modifying data. Basically, an auto-increment column means that the column is automatically assigned a numeric value, in ascending sequence, as each row is added to the table. Auto-increment columns are often used with primary keys but can also be assigned to an ordinary column.

Note that the term *auto-increment* is specific to MySQL. Microsoft uses the term *identity* to refer to the same type of attribute.

DATABASE DIFFERENCES: Oracle

Oracle doesn't have an auto-increment type of attribute. Instead, Oracle requires you to define a column as a *sequence* and then create a *trigger* to populate that column with sequential values. This procedure is beyond the scope of this book.

A fourth column attribute is whether or not the column is allowed to contain NULL values. The default is to allow NULL values. If you don't want to allow a column to contain NULLs, it is normally specified via a `NOT NULL` keyword applied to the column description.

The final column attribute we'll mention is whether the column is assigned a default value. A default value is one that is automatically assigned to the column if no value for that column is provided when a row is added. For example, if most of your customers are in the U.S., you may want to specify that a column containing a country code be given a default value of U.S.

Primary Keys and Indexes

Let's turn to the topic of primary keys and explain how that attribute relates to table indexes.

Indexes are a physical structure that can be added to any column in a database table. Indexes serve the purpose of speeding up data retrieval when that column is involved in a SQL statement. The actual data in the index is hidden, but basically the index involves a structure that maintains information on the sort order of the column, thus allowing for quicker retrieval when specific values are requested.

One downside to indexing a column is that it requires more disk storage in your database. A second negative is that indexes generally slow down data updates involving that column. This happens because any time a row is inserted or modified, the index must recalculate the proper sorted order for values in that column.

Any column can be indexed, but only one column can be designated as a primary key. Specifying a column as a primary key means two things: The column will be indexed, and the column will be guaranteed to contain unique values.

As discussed in Chapter 1, primary keys accomplish two main benefits for the database user: They enable you to uniquely identify a single row in a table, and they allow you to easily relate tables to one another. And now, you can add a third benefit: By being indexed, the primary key enables faster data retrieval of rows involving that column.

The main reason for having primary keys is to guarantee unique values for all rows in a table. There always has to be a way to identify single rows for updates or deletes, and the primary key ensures that can be done.

A primary key can actually span more than one column and can consist of two or three columns. If the primary key contains more than one column, it simply means that all those columns together will contain a unique value. This type of primary key is normally referred to as a *composite primary key.* As an example of when a composite primary key might be utilized, let's say that you have a Movies table. You'd like to have a key that uniquely defines each movie in the table. Rather than use a MovieID integer value as the key, you'd like to use the movie title as the key. The problem, however, is that movies are sometimes remade with the same title. To solve the problem, you can use two columns, the movie title and the year, to form a composite primary key to uniquely define each movie.

Because primary keys must contain unique values, they are never allowed to contain NULL values. Some value for the column must always be specified.

Finally, primary keys are often specified as auto-increment columns. By making a primary key auto-increment, database developers don't need to worry about assigning a unique value for the column. The auto-increment feature takes care of that requirement.

Foreign Keys

SQL databases also designate specific columns as a foreign key. A foreign key is simply a reference from a column in one table to a column in a different table. When setting up a foreign key, you will be asked to specify both columns. The foreign key column in the table being configured is often referred to as being in the *child table.* The referenced column in the other table is referred to as being in the *parent table.*

For example, let's say you have a Customers table with a CustomerID column that is set up as a primary key. You also have an Orders table with an OrderID column set up as a primary key and a CustomerID column. You would like to set up the CustomerID column in the Orders table as a foreign key that references the CustomerID column in the Customer table. In this case, the Orders table is the child table and the Customers table is the parent table.

When you set up foreign keys, you will be able to set some specific actions for updates and deletes involving rows in the parent table. The three most common actions are:

- No Action
- Cascade
- Set Null

Let's continue with the example of the Customers and Orders tables. The most common action to specify is No Action. This is the default action if none is specified. If you set the CustomerID column in the Orders table to No Action for updates, that means that a check is made whenever an update is attempted in the parent table on the CustomerID column. If it tries to do an update on the CustomerID, which would result in any row in the child pointing to a value that no longer exists, it will prevent that action from occurring. The same would be true if No Action is specified for deletes. This ensures that, when using the CustomerID column in both tables, all rows in the Orders properly point to an existing row in the Customers table.

The second alternative for a specified action for foreign keys is Cascade. This means that when a value in the parent table is updated, and if that value affects rows in the child table, then it will automatically update all rows in the child table to reflect the new value in the parent table. Similarly, if a row in the parent table is deleted, and if that affects rows in the child table, it will automatically delete affected rows in the child table.

A third alternative for a specified action for foreign keys is Set Null, which means that when a value in the parent is updated or deleted, and if that values affects rows in the child table, it will automatically update all affected rows in the child table to contain a NULL value in the foreign key.

Creating Tables

The `CREATE TABLE` statement can be used to create new tables in a database. The syntax and available features vary among databases. We're going to focus on a simple example that creates a table with these attributes:

- The table name is MyTable.
- The first column in the table is named ColumnOne and defined as a primary key. This column will be defined as an `INT` (integer) datatype and also as an auto-increment column.
- The second column in the table is named ColumnTwo and defined as an `INT` datatype. This column will not allow NULL values. This column will also be defined as a foreign key, with No Action specified for both deletes and updates, related to a column named FirstColumn in another table called RelatedTable.

- The third column in the table is named ColumnThree and defined as a VARCHAR datatype with a length of 25. This column will allow NULL values.
- The fourth column in the table is named ColumnFour and defined as a FLOAT datatype and will allow NULL values. It will be given a default value of 10.

Here is the CREATE TABLE statement in Microsoft SQL Server that accomplishes this:

```
CREATE TABLE MyTable
(ColumnOne INT IDENTITY (1,1) PRIMARY KEY NOT NULL,
ColumnTwo INT NOT NULL
REFERENCES RelatedTable (FirstColumn),
ColumnThree VARCHAR (25) NULL,
ColumnFour FLOAT NULL DEFAULT (10) )
```

DATABASE DIFFERENCES: MySQL and Oracle

The same CREATE TABLE statement in MySQL looks like:

```
CREATE TABLE MyTable
ColumnOne INT AUTO_INCREMENT PRIMARY KEY NOT NULL
ColumnTwo INT NOT NULL,
ColumnThree VARCHAR (25) NULL,
ColumnFour FLOAT NULL DEFAULT 10,
CONSTRAINT FOREIGN KEY (ColumnTwo)
REFERENCES 'RelatedTable' (FirstColumn) );
```

The same statement in Oracle is:

```
CREATE TABLE MyTable
(ColumnOne INT PRIMARY KEY NOT NULL
ColumnTwo INT NOT NULL,
ColumnThree VARCHAR2 (25) NULL,
ColumnFour FLOAT DEFAULT 10 NULL,
CONSTRAINT "ForeignKey" FOREIGN KEY (ColumnTwo)
REFERENCES RelatedTable (FirstColumn) );
```

As previously mentioned, Oracle doesn't allow for auto-increment columns.

After a table is created, an ALTER TABLE statement can be used to modify specific attributes of the table. Due to its complexity and to the vast differences between databases, the syntax for the ALTER TABLE won't be covered in this book.

As one example, if you wanted to modify MyTable to eliminate the ColumnThree column from the table, you would need to issue this ALTER TABLE statement:

```
ALTER TABLE MyTable
DROP COLUMN ColumnThree
```

The syntax for deleting a table is simple. To delete MyTable, issue this statement:

```
DROP TABLE MyTable
```

Creating Indexes

SQL provides a CREATE INDEX statement to create indexes after the table is created. You can also use the ALTER TABLE statement to add or modify indexes.

If you would like to add a new index on the ColumnFour column in MyTable table, the syntax in Microsoft SQL Server is:

```
CREATE INDEX Index2
ON MyTable (ColumnFour)
```

This creates a new index named index2.

To delete an index, simply issue a DROP INDEX statement such as:

```
DROP INDEX Index2
ON MyTable
```

DATABASE DIFFERENCES: Oracle

In Oracle, the equivalent DROP INDEX statement is:

```
DROP INDEX Index2;
```

Looking Ahead

The SQL statements that add or modify tables and indexes are complex but relatively unimportant to learn in detail. Database software generally provides graphical tools to modify the structure of tables without having to resort to issuing SQL statements. The important concepts to take from this chapter are a knowledge of the various table attributes, including an understanding of how indexes and primary and foreign keys are related to each other.

In our next chapter, "Principles of Database Design," we move from the relatively mundane task of creating tables to the much broader topic of database design. Just as tables are normally created before their data is accessed, it's also true that databases are normally designed before tables are created in those databases. So in a sense, we're moving in reverse through topics that are normally introduced before data retrieval is ever attempted. The specific design of your database is, of course, an essential component of your ability to deliver quality results via SQL. If a database is poorly designed, you're going to be hindered in your subsequent attempts to retrieve data. Basic knowledge of the database design principles discussed in the next chapter can go a long way toward ensuring a quality database environment.

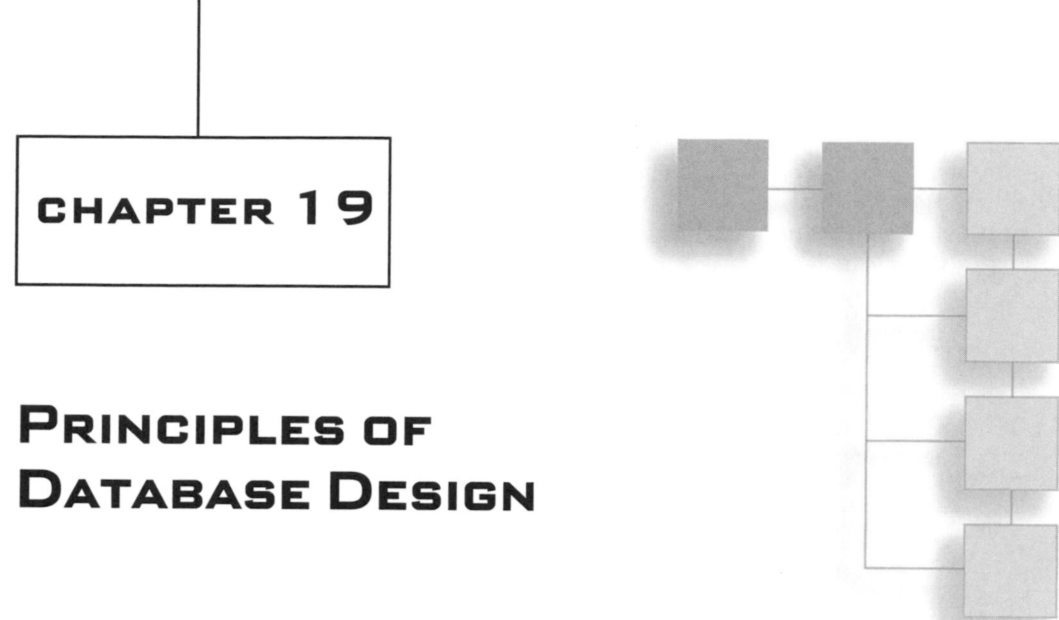

Chapter 19

Principles of Database Design

In our first chapter, we introduced the notion that relational databases are a collection of data, stored in any number of tables. The tables are assumed to be related to each other in some fashion. In the prior chapter on maintaining tables, we made clear that database designers can, if they want, assign foreign keys to ensure that certain relationships between tables are maintained properly.

However, even with our knowledge of primary and foreign keys, we still have not yet addressed the basic issue of how to design a database in the first place. The main questions to address are the following:

- How should data be organized into a set of related tables?
- What data elements should be placed in each table?

Once tables and their data elements are defined, then a database administrator can go about the business of creating foreign keys, indexes, appropriate datatypes, and so on.

There will never be a single correct answer to the above two questions. Besides the fact that every organization or business is unique, it is also true that there is no definitive solution for any given business. Much depends on how flexible a business wants its data design to be. Another obvious factor is the existence of current data. Very few organizations have the luxury of designing their databases in a vacuum, apart from what already exists.

Despite these provisos, certain database design principles have evolved over time to guide us in our quest for an optimal design structure. It should be said from the outset that the most influential architect of relational database design is E.F. Codd, who published his groundbreaking article, "A Relational Model of Data for Large Shared Data Banks" in 1970. This article laid the foundation for what we now call the *relational model* and the concept of *normalization.*

Goals of Normalization

The term *normalization* refers to a specific process that allows designers to turn unstructured data into a properly designed set of tables and data elements.

The best way to understand normalization is to illustrate what it isn't. To do this, we'll start with the presentation of a poorly designed table with a number of obvious problems. The following is a table named Grades, and it attempts to present information about all of the grades that students have received for the tests they've taken. Each row represents a grade for a particular student.

Test	Student	Date	Total Points	Grade	TestFormat	Teacher	Assistant
Pronoun Quiz	Amy	2009-03-02	10	8	Multiple Choice	Smith	Collins
Pronoun Quiz	Jon	2009-03-02	10	6	Multiple Choice	Jones	Brown
Solids Quiz	Beth	2009-03-03	20	17	Multiple Choice	Kaplan	NULL
China Test	Karen	2009-02-04	50	45	Essay	Harris	Taylor
China Test	Alex	2009-03-04	50	38	Essay	Harris	Taylor
Grammar Test	Karen	2009-03-05	100	88	Multiple Choice, Essay	Smith	Collins

Let's first list the information that each column in this table is meant to provide. The columns are:

- **Test:** A description of the test or quiz given
- **Student:** The student who took the test
- **Date:** The date on which the test was taken
- **TotalPoints:** The total number of possible points for the test
- **Grade:** The number of points that the student received

- **TestFormat:** The format of the test, either essay, multiple choice, or both
- **Teacher:** The teacher who gave the test
- **Assistant:** The person who assisted the teacher in this class

We're going to assume that the primary key for this table is a composite primary key consisting of the Test and Student columns. Each row in the table is meant to express a grade for a specific test and student.

Let's now discuss two obvious problems with this table. First, certain data is unnecessarily duplicated. For example, you can see that the Pronoun Quiz, which was given on 2009-03-02, had a total of 10 points. The problem, however, is that this information needs to be repeated on every row for that quiz. It would be better if we could simply record the total points for that particular quiz once.

A second problem is that data is repeated within certain single cells. We have a row for which the TestFormat is both Multiple Choice and Essay. This was done because the test had both types of questions. But this makes the data difficult to utilize. If we wanted to retrieve all tests with essay questions, how could we do that?

To be more general, the main problem with this table is that it attempts to put all information into a single table. It would be much better to break down the information in this table into separate entities, such as students, grades, and teachers, representing each entity as a separate table. The power of SQL can then be used to join tables together to retrieve any needed information.

With this discussion in mind, let's now formalize what the process of normalization hopes to accomplish. There are two main goals:

- **Eliminate redundant data.** The above example clearly illustrates the issue of redundant data. But why is this important? What exactly is the problem with listing the same data on multiple rows? Besides the obvious duplication of effort, one answer is that redundancy reduces flexibility. When data is repeated, that means that any changes to particular values affect multiple rows rather than just one.

- **Eliminate insert, delete, and update anomalies.** The problem of redundant data also relates to this second goal, which is to eliminate insert, delete, and update anomalies. Let's say, for example, that one particular teacher gets married and changes her name. You would like the data to reflect the new name. You now need to do an update on all rows that contain her name. Because the data is stored redundantly, you need to update a large amount of data, rather than just one row.

There are also insert and delete anomalies. For example, let's say you just hired a new teacher to teach music. You would like to record that somewhere in your database. However, since that teacher hasn't yet given any tests, there is nowhere to put this information, since you don't have a table specific to the entity of teachers.

Similarly, a delete anomaly would occur if you wanted to delete a row, but by doing so that would eliminate some related piece of information. To use another example, if you had a database of books and wanted to delete a row for a book by Nathaniel Hawthorne, and if that were the only book for Mr. Hawthorne, then that row deletion would not only eliminate the book, but also the fact that Nathanial Hawthorne is an author of other books you might acquire in the future.

How to Normalize Data

We've been throwing around the term *normalization* for a while. It's now time to be more specific about what it means.

The term itself originates with E.F. Codd, and it refers to a series of recommended steps taken to remove redundancy and update anomalies from a database design. The steps involved in the normalization process are commonly referred to as *first normal form, second normal form, third normal form,* and so on. Although certain individuals have described steps up to *sixth normal form,* the usual practice is to go only through first, second, and third normal form. When data is in third normal form, it is generally said to be sufficiently normalized.

We are not going to describe the entire set of rules and procedures for converting data into first, second, and third normal form. There are texts that will lead you through the process in great detail, showing you how to transform data first into first normal form, then into second form, and then finally into third normal form.

Instead, we are going to summarize the rules for getting your data into third normal form. In practice, an experienced database administrator can jump from unstructured data to third normal form without having to follow every intermediate procedure. We will do the same thing here.

The three main rules for normalizing your data are as follows:

- **Eliminate repeating data.** This rule means that no multivalued attributes are allowed. In the previous example, we cannot allow a value such as Multiple Choice, Essay to exist in a single data cell. The existence of multiple values in a single cell creates obvious difficulties in retrieving data by any given specified value.

  A corollary to this rule is that repeated columns are not allowed. In our example, the database might have been designed so that, rather than a single column named TestFormat, we had two separate columns named Test Format1 and TestFormat2. With this alternative approach, we might have placed the value Multiple Choice in the Test Format1 column and Essay in the TestFormat2 column. This would not be permitted. We don't want to have repeated data, whether it is multiple values in a single column or multiple columns to handle similar data.

- **Eliminate partial dependencies.** This rule refers primarily to situations where the primary key for a table is a composite primary key, meaning a key composed of multiple columns. The rule states that no column in the table can be related only to part of the primary key.

  Let's illustrate with an example. As mentioned, the primary key in the Grades table is a composite key consisting of the Student and Test columns. The problem occurs with columns such as TotalPoints. The TotalPoints column is really an attribute of the test and has nothing to do with students. This rule mandates that all non-key columns in a table refer to the entire key, and not just a part of the key. In essence, partial dependencies indicate that the data in the table relates to more than one entity.

- **Eliminate transitive dependencies.** This rule refers to situations where a column in the table refers not to the primary key, but to another non-key column in the same table. In this example, the Assistant column is really an attribute of the Teacher column. The fact that Assistant relates to the teacher and not to anything in the primary key (test or student) indicates that the information doesn't belong in this table.

So we've seen the problems and have talked about the rules for fixing the data. How are proper database design changes actually determined? This is where experience comes in. And there is generally not a single solution to the problem.

That said, the following is one solution to this design problem. In this new design, several tables have been created from the one original table, and all data is now in normalized form. Figure 19.1 shows the tables in the new design, shown without data.

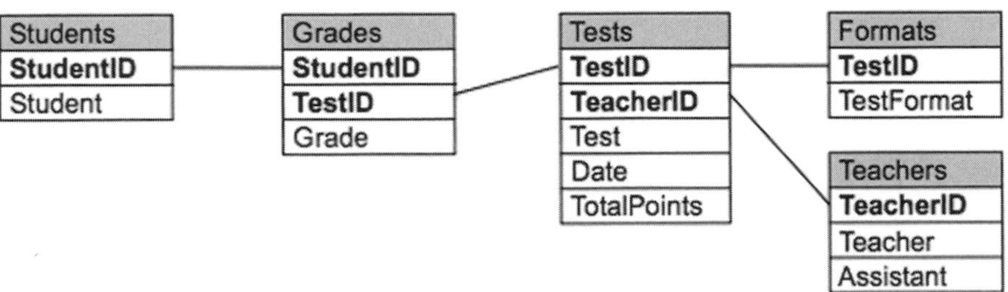

Figure 19.1
Normalized design.

The primary keys in each table are shown in bold. A number of ID columns with auto-increment values have been added to the tables, allowing relationships between the tables to be defined. All the other columns are the same as shown before.

The main point to notice is that every entity discussed in this example has been broken out into separate tables. The Students table has information about each student. The only attribute in this table is the student name. The Grades table has information about each grade. It has a composite primary key of StudentID and TestID because each grade is tied to a student and to a specific test given.

The Tests table has information about each test given, such as the date, TeacherID, the test description, and the total points for the test

The Formats table has information about the test formats. Multiple rows are added to this table for each test, to show whether the test is multiple choice, essay, or both.

The Teachers table has information about each teacher, including the teacher's assistant, if there is one.

The following shows the data contained in these new tables, corresponding to the data in the original Grades table.

Students table:

StudentID	Student
1	Amy
2	Jon
3	Beth
4	Karen
5	Alex

Teachers table:

TeacherID	Teacher	Assistant
1	Smith	Collins
2	Jones	Brown
3	Kaplan	NULL
4	Harris	Taylor

Tests table:

TestID	TeacherID	Test	Date	TotalPoints
1	1	Pronoun Quiz	2009-03-02	10
2	2	Pronoun Quiz	2009-03-02	10
3	3	Solids Quiz	2009-03-03	20
4	4	China Test	2009-03-04	50
5	1	Grammar Test	2009-03-05	100

Formats table:

TestID	TestFormat
1	Multiple Choice
2	Multiple Choice
3	Multiple Choice
4	Essay
5	Multiple Choice
5	Essay

Grades table:

StudentID	TestID	Grade
1	1	8
2	2	6
3	3	17
4	4	45
5	4	38
4	5	88

Your first impression might be that we have unnecessarily complicated the situation, rather than improved it. For example, the Grades table is now a mass of numbers, the meaning of which is not completely obvious on quick inspection.

This is true. However, remembering the ability of SQL to join tables together easily, you can also see that there is now much greater flexibility in this new design. Not only are we free to join together only those tables needed for any particular analysis, but we can now add new columns to these tables much more readily, without affecting anything else.

Our information has become more modularized. For example, if we should decide that we want to capture additional information about each student, such as address and phone, we can simply add new columns to the Students table. Additionally, when we want to modify a student's address or phone later, it only affects one row in the table

The Art of Database Design

Ultimately, designing a database is much more than simply going through the normalization procedures. Database design is really more of an art than a science, and it requires asking and thinking about relevant business issues.

In our grades example, we presented one possible database design as an illustration of how to normalize data. In truth, there are many possibilities for designing this database. Much depends on the realities of how the data will be accessed and modified. Numerous questions can be asked to ascertain whether your design is as flexible and meaningful as it needs to be. For example:

- **Are there other tables that need to be added to our database?** One obvious choice would be a Subjects table, so you could easily select tests by subject, such as English or Math. If you did this, would you relate the subject to the test or to the teacher who gave the test?

- **Is it possible for a grade to count in more than one subject?** Maybe the English and Social Studies teachers are doing a combined lesson and want certain tests to count for both subjects. How do you account for that?
- **What do you do if a child flunks a grade and is now taking the same tests for a second year?** How do you differentiate his grade now from last year's grades?
- **How do you allow for special rules that teachers might implement, such as dropping the lowest quiz score in a particular time period?**
- **Are there special analysis requirements for the data?** If there is more than one teacher for the same subject, do you want to be able to compare the average grades for the students of each teacher, to make sure that one teacher isn't unfairly inflating grades?

The list of possible questions is endless. But the point is that data doesn't exist in a vacuum. There is a necessary interaction between data design and requirements in the real world. Databases need to be designed in such a way as to allow for needed flexibility. However, there is also a danger that databases can be overly designed to a point where the data becomes unintelligible. A zealous database administrator may decide to create 20 tables to allow for every possible situation. That, too, is inadvisable. Database design is something of a balancing act in search of a design that is sufficiently flexible but also intuitive and understandable by users of the system.

Alternatives to Normalization

We have emphasized that normalization is the overriding principle that should be followed in designing a database. In certain situations, however, there are viable alternatives that might make more sense.

For example, in the realm of data warehouse systems and software, many practitioners advocate utilizing a *star schema* design for databases rather than normalization. In a star schema, a certain amount of redundancy is allowed and encouraged. The emphasis is on creating a data structure that more intuitively reflects business realities, and also one that allows for quick processing of data by special analytical software.

To give a brief overview of star schema designs, the main idea is to create a central fact table, which is related to any number of dimension tables. The fact table contains all the quantitative numbers that are additive in nature. In our prior example, the Grade column is such a number, since we can add up grades to obtain a meaningful total grade. The dimension tables contain information on all the entities that are related to the central facts, such as subject, time, teacher, student, and so on.

Furthermore, special analytical software exists that allows database developers to create cubes from their star schema databases. These cubes extend analysis capabilities, allowing users to drill down predefined hierarchies, which are defined in the various dimensions. A user of such a system would be able to drill down from viewing a semester's worth of grades for a student, to his grades in any individual week.

Figure 19.2 shows what a database with a star schema design might look like for our grades example.

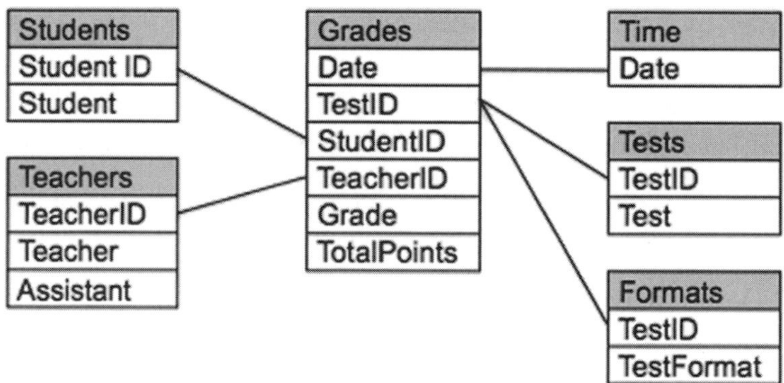

Figure 19.2
Star schema design.

In this design, the Grades table is the central fact table. The other tables are all dimension tables.

The first four columns in the Grades table (Date, TestID, StudentID, and TeacherID) are there only to relate the table to each of the dimensions. The other two columns have the additive numeric quantities we talked about. Notice that

TotalPoints is now in the Grades table. In our normalized design, it was an attribute of the Tests table. By putting both the Grade and TotalPoints in the Grades table, we can use our analytical software to easily sum up grades and compute average grades (Grade divided by the TotalPoints) for any set of data.

Certainly, this is only a brief introduction to the subject of designing databases for data warehouses. It illustrates the point that there are many different ways to design a database, and the best way often relates to the type of software that will be used with the data.

Looking Ahead

This chapter covered the principles of database design. We went over the basics of the normalization process, showing how a database with a single table can be converted into a more flexible structure with multiple tables, related by additional key columns. We also emphasized that database design is not merely a technical exercise. Attention must be paid to organizational realities and to considerations as to how the data will be utilized. Finally, we briefly described one alternative to the conventional normalized design, in an effort to emphasize that there is often more than one approach to this endeavor.

In our final chapter, "Strategies for Displaying Data," we're going to discuss some interesting possibilities for using reporting software tools to complement our knowledge of SQL. In our quest to sharpen our SQL skills, we must not forget that there is a world beyond SQL. We make to make sure that we don't expend our efforts in SQL when the underlying objective can be accomplished more effectively through other means.

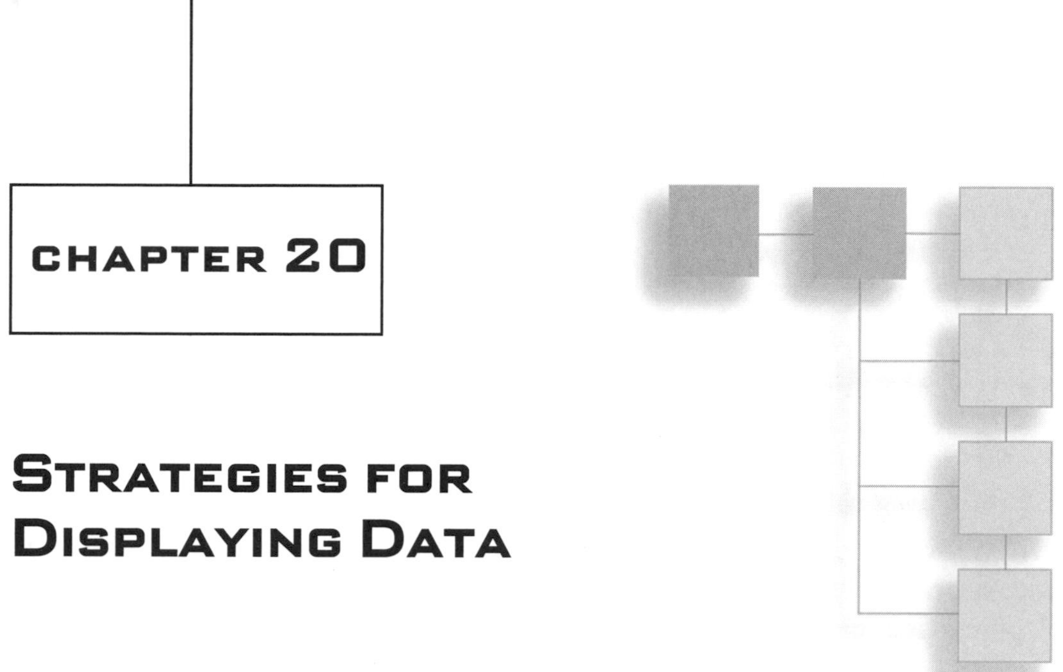

Chapter 20

Strategies for Displaying Data

In this final chapter, we're going to return to the main theme of this book, which is how to retrieve data from relational databases. In the past few chapters, we've taken a slight detour from the related topics of updating data, maintaining tables, and designing databases.

But now, we want to focus again on the role of SQL in retrieving data. More specifically, we want to address situations where data is presented to users via reporting software.

Beyond SQL

Specialized reporting tools are often used to present data to users. Examples of this type of software include Microsoft Reporting Services and Crystal Reports. These software packages allow developers to connect to databases via SQL, and they provide a well-designed user interface, allowing users to easily access data via predefined reports. With minimal effort, these reporting tools also enable developers to present data in a variety of formats.

In addition, most reporting tools enable users to export retrieved data to a spreadsheet, such as Excel. This provides opportunities for users to manipulate their own data, allowing them to transform data into formats unique to spreadsheets.

With this in mind, the purpose of this chapter is to raise an awareness on the part of the database developer of what can be accomplished either through reporting software or by users manipulating data in spreadsheets. Either way, there are opportunities for offloading some of the complexity that would ordinarily be involved with using SQL to other tools or the end user. Often, it is easier and better for the user to play a role in the final arrangement of data than it is for the database developer to attempt to do it all in SQL.

Basically, we'll consider the possibility of avoiding overly complex SQL statements when similar functionality can be handled either by a reporting tool or by the user viewing the data.

Reporting Tools and Crosstab Reports

We're going to use Microsoft Reporting Services to illustrate what can be done with reporting tools. This is just one of many available tools, including Crystal Reports, Cognos, and MicroStrategy.

Specifically, we're going to look at a report type that Microsoft calls a *matrix report.* Outside of Microsoft, matrix reports are commonly referred to as *crosstab reports.*

The simplest way to create a new report in Microsoft Reporting Services is through their Report Wizard. After being invoked, the wizard runs you through the following steps:

1. Obtain a data source and connection.
2. Create the query, either through a provided `SELECT` statement or by using a built-in Query Builder.
3. Specify a report type. Options include tabular and matrix.
4. Arrange specific columns from the `SELECT` or Query Builder into various report areas.
5. Select a visual style for the report.

Step 3 allows you to specify the report type. In Microsoft terminology, a *tabular report* presents data in the normal fashion. Data elements are shown as columns, and each occurrence appears as a new row. The data shown in the report is exactly as the `SELECT` statement or Query Builder specifies.

The matrix report is the new feature we want to consider. When the matrix report type is utilized, data items are not placed into columns as normal. Instead, data items are placed into one of four different areas of the report: rows, columns, details, and pages.

The best way to illustrate the difference between tabular and matrix reports is with a simple example. Let's say that you have a SELECT statement such as the following:

```
SELECT
CustomerName AS 'Customer',
ProductCategory AS 'Product Category',
OrderAmount AS 'Amount'
FROM SalesTable
```

When you create a tabular report with this statement, a report might appear as in Figure 20.1.

Customer	Product Category	Amount
Carter	Desks	150
Carter	Paper	5
Kraft	Chairs	120
Pollen	Chairs	40
Pollen	Chairs	200
Smith	Chairs	40
Smith	Desks	300

Figure 20.1
Tabular report.

Data in this tabular report is presented in the normal arrangement of columns and rows.

Now, let's see what the report looks like if the same SELECT statement is used in conjunction with a matrix report. In specifying the matrix report, the CustomerName column can be put in the rows area, ProductCategory in the columns area, and OrderAmount in the details area. Figure 20.2 displays the resulting matrix report.

	Chairs	Desks	Paper
Carter	0	150	5
Kraft	120	0	0
Pollen	240	0	0
Smith	40	300	0

Figure 20.2
Matrix report.

The matrix report presents data in an entirely different way. Rather than showing individual rows, it summarizes the data by customer and product groups. The report has dynamically determined which unique values exist in the customers and product groups, and it presents the necessary rows and columns to display all the values.

The details area of a matrix report requires data items with quantitative values, because those values will be summed up automatically in the matrix report. Notice that in the tabular report, Pollen, had two orders of chairs, one for 40 and one for 200. In the matrix report, these two values were summed automatically, to display a total of 240.

There are, of course, numerous other features and capabilities of this and other reporting tools. The main point is to remain mindful of what can accomplished with reporting tools to lessen the burden on the developer writing SQL statements.

Spreadsheets and Pivot Tables

In addition to reporting tools, spreadsheets also provide a great deal of functionality for you to manipulate data. Most reporting tools allow you to export data into an Excel spreadsheet. At that point, you have the ability to do whatever you want in Excel to format and analyze the data.

Many basic Excel functions and features overlap what can be specified in a `SELECT` statement. For example, Excel allows you to sort data easily. Excel provides numerous built-in functions that are similar or identical to the built-in functions in SQL.

Another important feature of Excel is the capability to group data with subtotals. This means that if you need both detailed data and subtotals by group, you can easily accomplish this in Excel. The SQL developer may need to provide data at only the lowest level of detail. With a few keystrokes in Excel, you can then group data and add subtotals as desired.

However, the most significant feature that Excel provides in this regard is the pivot table. With Excel, you have the ability to select any area of data on a worksheet and convert that data into a pivot table. At a basic level, a pivot table is the equivalent of the matrix (crosstab) report type seen in the previous example.

However, the pivot table also adds some key elements that greatly enhance its usefulness:

- **First, a pivot table is completely interactive.** Rather than viewing a static crosstab report, the user can modify the pivot table quickly by rearranging data elements into the various areas: rows, columns, and data. In addition, pivot tables provide a fourth data area called the *page,* which allows for data items to be used in filtering but not displayed.
- **The data in pivot tables exists as a separate store of data and can even be saved as a separate file.** Because the data in a pivot table exists on its own, users can rearrange the data without affecting the data from which the pivot table was created.
- **Pivot tables allow for additional data selection.** For example, specific values of various data items can be excluded. Or the aggregated values in the data area of the pivot table can be changed from sums to counts.
- **Pivot tables can add drill-down functionality to the data.** For example, if the underlying data contains columns such as country, state, and city, the pivot table can be set up so you can double-click on a country to see all states in that country and then double-click again to see all cities in each state.
- **Pivot tables allow users to drill through from summarized data to the underlying details.** Thus, you have the ability to double-click on any individual value in the data area to see the individual rows that contributed to that number.

It's beyond the scope of this book to explore pivot tables in any amount of detail. But an awareness of what you can accomplish with pivot tables can be very useful for the SQL developer.

Figure 20.3 shows an example of a pivot table that was created from the same data as listed earlier, but with the addition of two new columns: Date and Subcategory. The Subcategory column is a further breakdown of the product category. In this pivot table, the date, product category, and subcategory were all put in the rows area. This illustrates how pivot tables can provide a further breakdown of data in a very flexible manner.

Sum of Amount			Customer			
Date	Product Category	Subcategory	Carter	Kraft	Pollen	Smith
12/5/2009	Chairs	Metal		120		40
		Plastic			40	
	Paper	Glossy	5			
12/6/2009	Desks	Wood	150			
12/7/2009	Chairs	Metal			200	
	Desks	Metal				300
Grand Total			155	120	240	340

Figure 20.3
Pivot table.

The important point about this pivot table is that there are three different levels of groups in the rows. First, it divides all data by date, then by product category, and finally by subcategory. You can see that on 12/5/09, there were two different product categories sold: chairs and paper. For chairs, there were two different subcategories sold: metal and plastic. For each of these categories, the pivot table provides a breakdown of sales by customer.

As such, pivot tables are very adept at summarizing data in innumerable ways. Additionally, users have the ability to arrange data items in almost any desired format.

Looking Ahead

In this chapter, we've examined a few ways in which reporting tools and spreadsheets can be used to display data in custom formats. In particular, the crosstab report adds an ability to summarize data in a way that is difficult to present strictly through SQL statements. Pivot tables in Excel utilize the basic concept of the crosstab report and extend it to provide additional flexibility and functionality for users. By being aware of reporting and user tools available to reformat data, SQL developers can focus their talents more productively on retrieving data and let the reporting tool or user handle more complex display issues.

Now that you've completed the book, why not try out a few commands on your own? If you haven't already done so, take a look at Appendices A, B, and C to get some tips on how to get started with Microsoft SQL Server, MySQL, or Oracle. These appendices provide instructions on how to install the free versions of these databases, and they also provide some basic information on how to use the software to execute SQL commands.

Finally, I sincerely hope that this book has served as a useful guide into the world of SQL. At the start of the book, I mentioned that SQL involves both logic and language. The language component is fairly obvious. In each chapter, I've stressed the keywords that are introduced and the meaning behind those words. But now that you've completed the book, I hope you can appreciate that the power of SQL is with the logic that it encompasses.

It is pure logic that allows you take a bunch of values arranged in columns and rows and transform it into something approaching information. The challenge in using SQL is in determining how to apply logic to real-world data. This is where the theoretical and practical meet. In using functions, aggregation, joins, subqueries, views, and the like, you'll grapple with the reality of raw data and learn how to manipulate it with a few twists of logic.

But logic isn't the end of the matter. The language of SQL plays an equally important role. I would say that the real beauty of SQL lies in the fact that the language is quite sparse. It's neither cryptic nor verbose. Each keyword has a distinct purpose and specifies a particular bit of logic and nothing more. I wouldn't go so far as to say that SQL has poetic qualities, but within the realm of computer languages, the language has a certain aesthetic appeal.

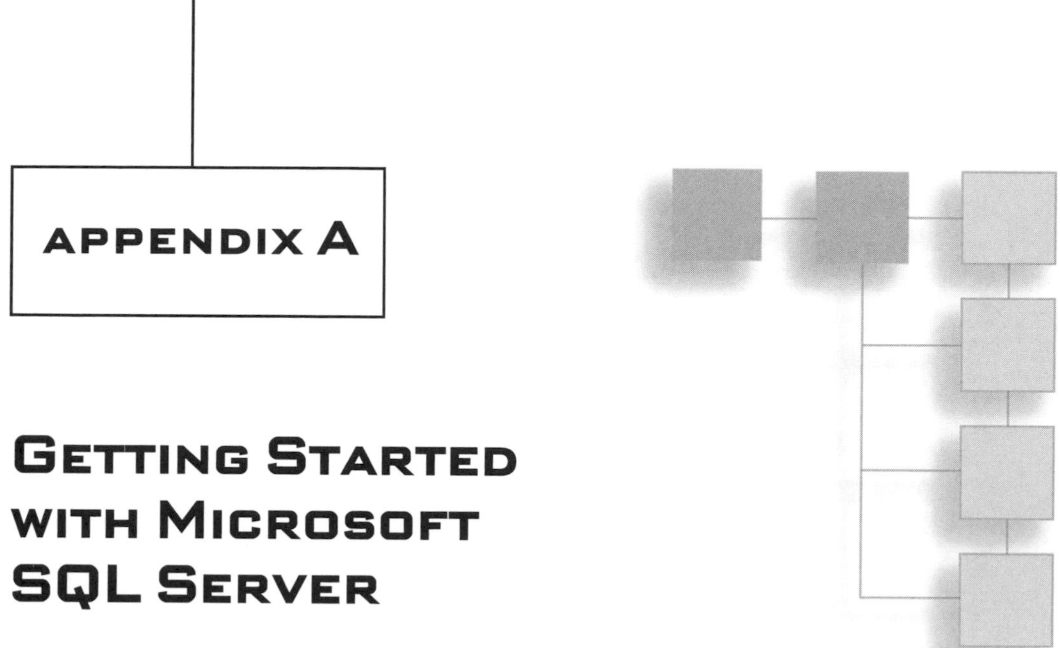

APPENDIX A

Getting Started with Microsoft SQL Server

Overview

The procedure to install the free version of Microsoft SQL Server is as follows. This procedure was tested on a PC with the Windows 7 operating system. Please note that the specific instructions may vary from what is shown here, depending on what is already installed on your PC.

As these procedures may change over time, please consult www.courseptr.com/downloads for any updates.

There are two main steps involved:

- Install SQL Server Express 2008
- Install SQL Server Management Studio

Microsoft SQL Server Express 2008 allows you to create databases. The SQL Server Management Studio is a graphical interface that allows you to issue SQL commands to interact with the server and any databases you create.

Both downloads are available at www.microsoft.com/sqlserver.

Installing SQL Server Express 2008

The steps for installing the Microsoft SQL Server database are as follows.

1. Go to www.microsoft.com/sqlserver.

2. In the Downloads area at the far right, click on SQL SERVER 2008 EXPRESS.
3. Click the INSTALL button.
4. If you don't already have it, a new window will pop up to allow you to install the Microsoft Web Platform. Click on the GET THE MICROSOFT WEB PLATFORM button.
5. You may then be asked a series of questions, such as if you want to run the application and allow various procedures to execute. Respond RUN, YES, or ALLOW to all questions.
6. After the install of Microsoft Web Platform completes, you will see a screen asking you to install SQL Server Express 2008. Click the INSTALL button.
7. On the License screen, click the ALLOW button.
8. On the Authentication Mode screen, select Mixed Mode authentication and enter a password for the SQL Server Administrator (SA) user.
9. After the install completes, click the FINISH and then the EXIT buttons.

After this has completed, you will have the following software installed:

- Microsoft SQL Server 2008 Import and Export Data
- Microsoft SQL Server 2008 Configuration Tools

Installing SQL Server Management Studio

The steps for installing the Microsoft SQL Server 2008 Express Management Tools are as follows:

1. Go to www.microsoft.com/sqlserver.
2. In the Downloads area, click on SQL SERVER 2008 EXPRESS.
3. On the grid under Other Installation Options, click the INSTALL button under the Management Tools column.
4. You may then be asked a series of questions, asking if you want to allow various procedures to execute. Respond YES or ALLOW to all questions.

5. You will now see a screen asking you to install SQL Server 2008 Management Studio Express. Click the INSTALL button.
6. On the License screen, click the I ACCEPT button. The software will then be installed. During the installation, you may see a window warning of compatibility issues. If so, click the RUN PROGRAM button.
7. After the install completes, click the EXIT button.

After this has completed, you will have the following software installed:

- Microsoft SQL Server Management Studio
- Microsoft SQL Server Integration Services

Using SQL Server Management Studio

When you start SQL Server Management Studio, you'll see a window to establish a connection with the Microsoft SQL Server that you already installed. Enter "localhost\SQLEXPRESS" in the Server Name box. In the Authentication box, select WINDOWS AUTHENTICATION. You don't need to enter a user name or password. Click the CONNECT button.

After connecting, you'll need to create a database to work with. To do this, find the Object Explorer pane on the left side of the window. Right-click on the DATABASES line and then select NEW DATABASE. In the New Database window, enter a name in the Database Name box (for example, FirstDatabase). Click the OK button. You will now see your new database under Databases.

To execute any desired SQL code, you can highlight your database and then click the NEW QUERY button. A new query window will open. You can enter any SQL code and then click the EXECUTE button. If you enter multiple SQL statements in the query window, you can highlight any number of individual statements and execute only the highlighted portion. The results of your query will be shown in either a Results or a Message pane after the query is executed. If there is data to be shown, it will appear in a Results pane. Otherwise, a status message will appear in a Message pane.

Microsoft provides complete online documentation on SQL Server in the MSDN (Microsoft Development Network) area of their Web site. The starting point for the Transact-SQL reference guide is currently at:

http://msdn.microsoft.com/en-us/library/bb510741.aspx

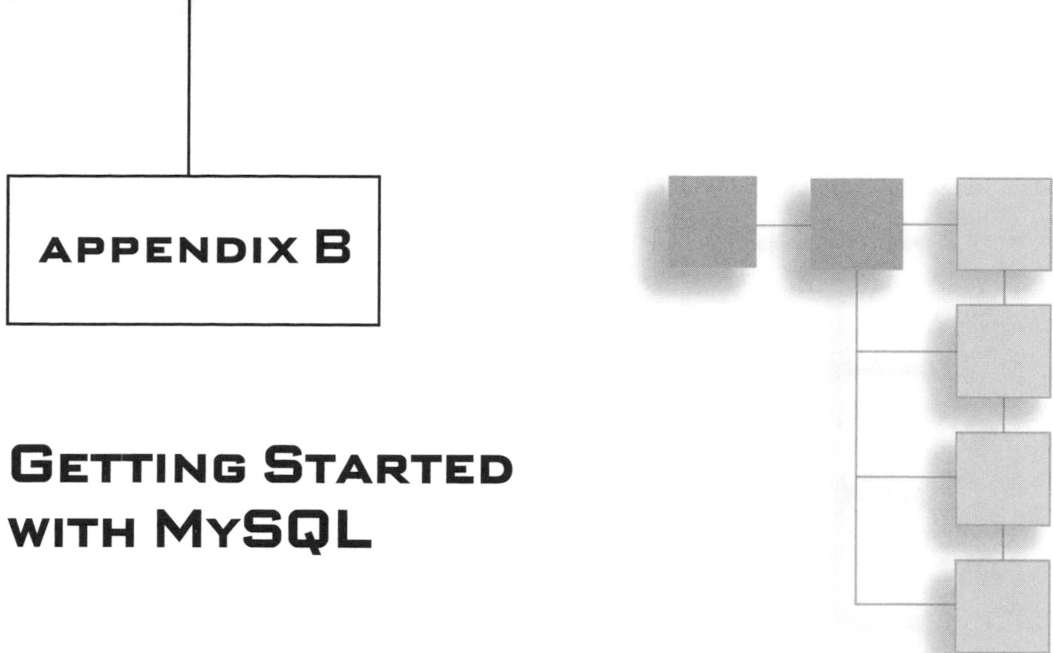

Appendix B

Getting Started with MySQL

Overview

The procedure to install the free version of MySQL is as follows. This procedure was tested on a PC with the Windows 7 operating system. Please note that the specific instructions may vary from what is shown below, depending on what is already installed on your PC.

As these procedures may change over time, please consult www.courseptr.com/downloads for any updates.

There are two main steps involved:

- Install MySQL Community Server
- Install MySQL Workbench, version 5.2 or higher

MySQL Community Server allows you to create databases. The MySQL Workbench is a graphical interface that allows you to issue SQL commands to interact with the server and any databases you create.

The MySQL Community server download is available at www.mysql.com. At the time of this writing, the MySQL Workbench download is in transition. In order to use this tool to execute SQL statements, you will need to obtain version 5.2 or higher. At present, this version is available in beta at dev.mysql.com.

Installing MySQL Community Server

The steps for installing the MySQL Community Server are as follows:

1. Go to www.mysql.com.
2. Click on the DOWNLOADS tab.
3. Click on MySQL COMMUNITY SERVER.
4. Select the MICROSOFT WINDOWS platform.
5. Click one of the DOWNLOAD buttons.
6. If you're a returning user, log in. Otherwise, register as a new user.
7. Click on HTTP next to one of the mirror files shown.
8. When asked if you want to run or save the file, select the RUN button.
9. After the download completes, when asked if you want to run the software, select the RUN button. The install setup wizard will then start.
10. On the Welcome screen, click the NEXT button.
11. On the Setup Type screen, select TYPICAL and then click the NEXT button.
12. On the Ready to Install screen, click the INSTALL button.
13. On the User Account Control message box, click the YES button. The software will then be installed.
14. Close the MySQL Enterprise message box.
15. On the MySQL Server 5.1 Setup Wizard box, click the FINISH button.
16. On the User Account control message box, click the YES button.
17. On the Registration screen, enter your information and register, if desired.
18. Go to the MySQL Server Instance Configuration Wizard message box. You may need to minimize your browser to see this.
19. On the Welcome screen, click the NEXT button.

20. On the Configuration Type screen, select STANDARD CONFIGURATION and then click the NEXT button.
21. On the Windows Options screen, check INSTALL AS WINDOWS SERVICE and make sure that LAUNCH THE MYSQL SERVER AUTOMATICALLY is checked; then click the NEXT button.
22. On the Security Option screen, enter a root password, if desired, and then click the NEXT button.
23. On the Ready to Execute screen, click the EXECUTE button. It should display the messages: Configuration file created, Windows service MySQL installed, Service started successfully.
24. Click the FINISH button.

After this has completed, you will have the following software installed:

- MySQL Command Line Client
- MySQL Server Instance Config Wizard

Installing MySQL Workbench

The steps for installing the MySQL Workbench are as follows. Note that you need to be on version 5.2 or higher in order to execute SQL with the tool. At the time of publication, version 5.2 is only available as a beta release.

1. Go to dev.mysql.com.
2. Click on the DOWNLOADS tab.
3. Click MySQL WORKBENCH on the left pane.
4. Click on MySQL WORKBENCH. Make sure that it is version 5.2 or higher.
5. Select the MICROSOFT WINDOWS platform.
6. Click one of the DOWNLOAD buttons.
7. If you're a returning user, log in. Otherwise, register as a new user if desired.
8. Click on HTTP next to one of the mirror files shown.

9. When asked if you want to run or save the file, select the RUN button. The setup wizard will then start.
10. On the Welcome screen, click the NEXT button.
11. On the Setup Type screen, select COMPLETE and then click the NEXT button.
12. On the Ready to Install screen, click the INSTALL button.
13. On the Completion screen, click the FINISH button.

After this has completed, you will have the following software installed:

- MySQL Workbench version 5.2

Using MySQL Workbench

When you first open MySQL Workbench after the initial install, you will need to establish a connection to your MySQL Server instance that you already installed.

To create a connection, select MANAGE CONNECTIONS under the Database menu. Click the NEW button to add a new connection. Then enter a connection name (ex: MyConnection) and click the TEST CONNECTION button. Enter a password if you previously supplied one. Then click the CLOSE button.

After creating the connection, you'll need to create a database to work with. To do this, select QUERY DATABASE under the Database menu. Select the connection you just created and click the OK button. Enter a password if you previously supplied one. You will now see an SQL Editor pane on your screen. An Object Explorer area will appear on the left side of the pane. A SQL Statements area will appear on the right side. In the Object Explorer, right-click any database and select CREATE SCHEMA. Enter the name of your new database (ex: FirstDatabase) in the Name textbox. Click the APPLY button twice and then the FINISH button. You will now see your new database in the Object Explorer. Finally, using the Default drop-down box at the top of the Object Explorer, select your new database as the default database.

Now that a connection and database have been created, you can enter any desired SQL statement in the SQL Statements area of the SQL Editor pane. If you don't see the SQL Editor pane, go back and select Query Database under the

Database menu as described previously. As before, this will ask you to select a connection.

After entering a SQL statement in the SQL Statements area, click the EXECUTE button, which looks like a lightning bolt. If you enter multiple statements in the window, you can highlight one individual statement and execute only the highlighted portion.

The results of your query will be shown under an Output or Result pane after the query is executed. If there is data to be shown, it will appear in a Result pane. Otherwise, a status message will appear under an Output pane.

MySQL provides complete documentation on their database. The MySQL reference manual is currently at:

http://dev.mysql.com/doc/refman/5.1/en

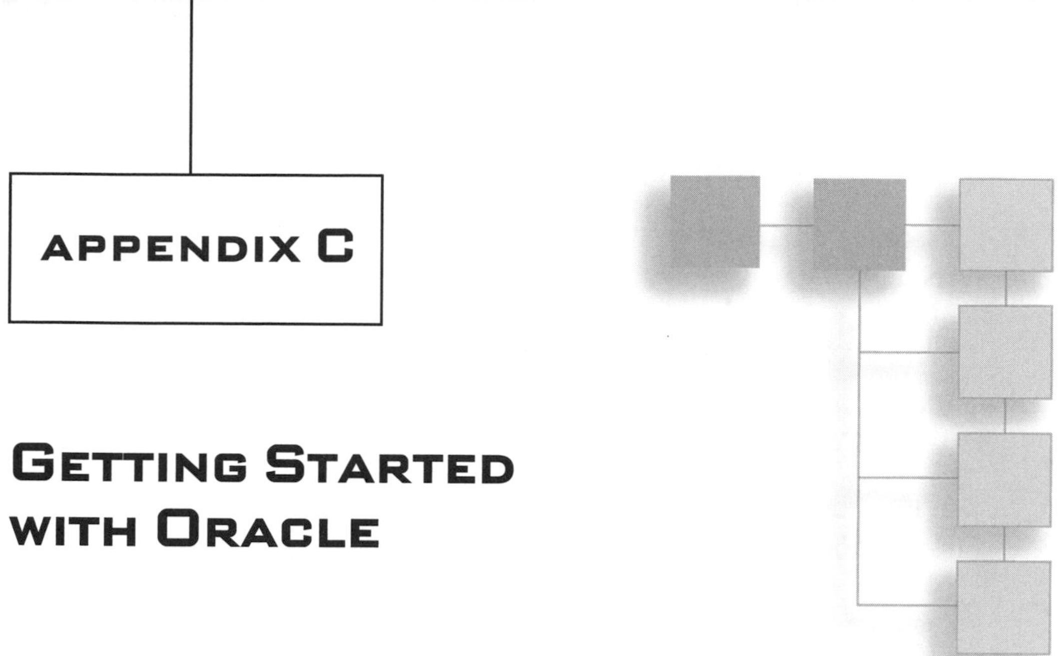

Appendix C

Getting Started with Oracle

Overview

The procedure to install the free version of Oracle Database is as follows. This procedure was tested on a PC with the Windows 7 operating system. Please note that the specific instructions may vary from what is shown below, depending on what is already installed on your PC.

As these procedures may change over time, please consult www.courseptr.com/downloads for any updates.

There is one step involved: Install Oracle Database Express Edition.

This installation will create a single database and provide a Web-based graphical interface that will allow you to execute SQL commands against the database.

This download is available at www.oracle.com/database.

As part of the install process, you may be asked to enter a database username. The name you should enter is SYSTEM.

Installing Oracle Database Express Edition

The steps for installing Oracle Database Express Edition are as follows.

1. Go to www.oracle.com/database.
2. Click on EXPRESS EDITION found on the left side of the page.

3. Click the FREE DOWNLOAD button.
4. Click ORACLE DATABASE 10g EXPRESS EDITION FOR MICROSOFT WINDOWS.
5. Click ACCEPT LICENSE AGREEMENT.
6. Under Oracle Database 10g Express Edition (Western European), click ORACLEXE.EXE.
7. You may then be asked a series of questions, asking if you want allow various procedures to execute. Respond RUN to all questions.
8. If you don't have an account with Oracle, click SIGN UP NOW. Otherwise, enter your username and password and then enter personal information.
9. When asked if you want to run or save the file, select the RUN button. The install setup wizard will then start.
10. On the Welcome screen, click the NEXT button.
11. On the License screen, click ACCEPT and then the NEXT button.
12. On the Destination screen, click the NEXT button.
13. On the Database Passwords screen, enter a password.
14. On Summary screen, click INSTALL.
15. After the install completes, click the FINISH button.

After this has completed, you will have the following software installed: Oracle Database 10g Express Edition.

The interface to the database is Web based. The various features are accessible under the Start menu under the Oracle Database 10g Express directory. The primary application in this directory that you'll want to use is Go To Database Home Page.

After the initial install, you will be taken to a Database Login screen on the Database Home Page. This is the same page you would enter by selecting GO TO DATABASE HOME PAGE under the Oracle Database 10g Express Edition directory under the Start menu.

After going to this Database Home Page, enter the user name SYSTEM and the password you created; then click the LOGIN button.

Using Oracle Database Express Edition

To gain access to the Oracle database, run the GO TO DATABASE HOME PAGE program under the Oracle Database 10g Express Edition directory in the start menu. This will open up a Web-based application, which will allow you to interface with the database.

To sign on, enter a username of SYSTEM, the password you specified during the install, and then click the LOGIN button.

You will then see four icons representing different functionalities: Administration, Object Browser, SQL, and Utilities. To execute SQL, click the SQL icon. You will then see three icons: SQL Commands, SQL Scripts, and Query Builder.

If you want to execute a single SQL statement, you can use the SQL Commands icon. This will allow you to execute a single command and see any results. If you enter multiple SQL statements, you can highlight one individual statement and execute only the highlighted portion. To execute a SQL statement in the SQL Commands window, click the RUN button.

If you want to execute multiple SQL statements, but you don't need to see the output, you can use the SQL Scripts icon. After selecting this icon, you can either create a new script or edit an existing script. To create a new script, click the CREATE button and then name the script and enter the statements you want in that script. To execute, click the RUN button. After you enter the request, it will ask for a confirmation to do the run. Click the RUN button again. You will then be able to see a summary of your script execution by clicking on the icon under the View Results column.

Oracle provides complete online documentation on their database. Their reference manuals are currently at:

http://www.oracle.com/pls/db112

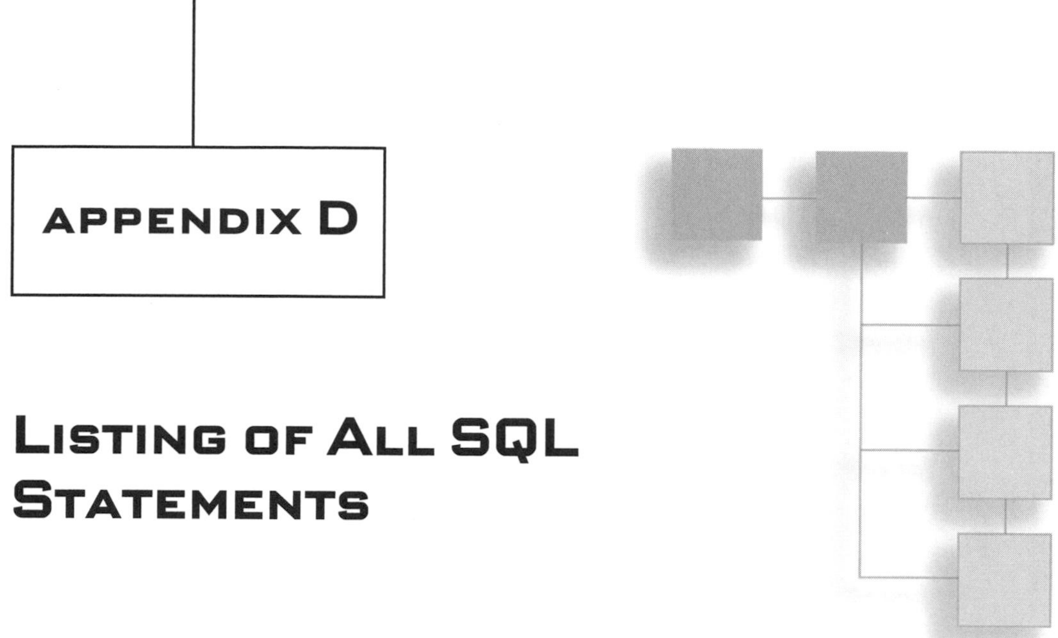

Listing of All SQL Statements

A listing of all SQL statements in this book can be found on this Cengage Web site: www.courseptr.com/downloads.

These three files are provided:

- SQL Statements and Data for SQL Server.doc
- SQL Statements and Data for MySQL.doc
- SQL Statements and Data for Oracle.doc

These three files list all SQL statements in the book for each of the three databases covered. Additionally, these files contain SQL scripts that allow you to create all the data used in the book. After running the setup scripts, you can execute any statement in the book and see the same output shown in the book.

Specific instructions on how to execute the setup scripts are provided in each of the files.

INDEX

Symbols

A

B

D

T

Maria T Eloniaga